Modern grandparenting

Games and activities to enjoy with your grandchildren

June Loves

FINCH PUBLISHING

SYDNEY

For my husband Max and my brother Ron:
both incredible grandfathers

Modern Grandparenting: Games and activities to enjoy with your grandchildren

First published in 2014 in Australia and New Zealand by Finch Publishing Pty Limited, ABN 49 057 285 248, Suite 2207, 4 Daydream Street, Warriewood, NSW, 2102, Australia.

14   8 7 6 5 4 3 2 1

There is a National Library of Australia Cataloguing-in-Publication entry available at the National Library.

Edited by Megan Drinan
Editorial assistance by Abigail Nathan
Text designed and typeset by Meg Dunworth
Cover design by Designerbility
Printed by Griffin Press

Finch titles can be viewed and purchased at www.finch.com.au

Contents

Introduction

Welcome to the world of grandparenting, a world that can be exciting, amazing and frequently challenging. Not so long ago my husband and I felt we were experienced, successful grandparents with ten much-loved grandchildren, who ranged in age from eighteen to 30. Then came along two great-grandchildren, a new grandson and a new granddog!

With the excitement and joy of the new arrivals came a reality check. In the years since we had first become grandparents society has changed dramatically and there have been many changes in attitudes and styles of parenting. Consequently for both experienced grandparents and brand new ones, there may be need for a 'refresher' course, and this is where *Modern Grandparenting* comes in.

Part One of this book is the result of gathering a collection of time-tested activities – some with a new twist – fun things to do and make. These activities are designed to shift our grandchildren away from TV, devices and computer screens, and encourage their imagination and creativity.

Part Two is a collection of helpful advice, hints and tips on all the issues that grandparents can face today, so you can thrive in the vital role of being a modern grandparent. Issues such as negotiating your relationships within your family, long-distance grandparenting, coping with new technology such as email, Skype and Facebook, essential and non-essential equipment, how to avoid burnout, the different stages of your grandchild's development and coping with school holidays are all covered.

Happy grandparenting!

Part one:

Things to make and do with your grandchildren

About this section

All it takes is a little planning and organisation to have a stress-free and happy time with your grandchildren. Search your memory for activities you enjoyed doing as a child and later with your own children. Choose old favourites and try some new ones.

The games and activities following will suit children between the ages of three and twelve years. Select the activities and games that match your grandchildren's interests and age groups – and your own physical ability, energy level and budget.

The activities, games, information and tips in Part One are divided into four sections:

1 **Indoor games and activities**, which are usually – but not always – quiet pastimes.
2 **Art and craft activities** can also be quiet, but messy. The key is to be prepared.
3 **Outdoor games and activities** are energetic, noisy and fun!
4 **Out and about** presents adventures, big and small, for you to tackle when you step outdoors with your grandchildren.

Begin by choosing the games and activities that suit your grandchildren's interests. Next, gradually introduce new activities that will challenge your grandchildren to use their imagination and creativity, building and extending their skills along the way. Consider planning around the seasons and the weather wherever you live. For example, spring is a great time for gardening and bird watching. Remember to always have a fall-back plan in case of a change in the weather.

By changing your equipment and materials, simple things to make and do with younger grandchildren can be transformed into more complicated activities for older grandchildren.

Recipes and eating tips are provided throughout this book and will help ensure you have a healthy, fun time with your grandchildren when preparing and providing their food and drinks.

Remember, if your game-plan collapses, you can always fall back on the rule of serendipity where good things happen by chance! Sometimes, simply tucking your grandchildren under your wing and involving them in your daily life can be the most rewarding activity of all.

Caution: Your supervision, care and common sense are essential at all times when spending time with your grandchildren.

Indoor games and activities

Introduction

Indoor games and activities are essential when skies are stormy, or when you or your grandchildren need some 'quiet' time. It's easy to provide starting points for imaginary play indoors and often, the simpler the better. Some textas can turn a big cardboard box into a stove, a temporary shop, pirate ship or cubby house, providing hours of (hopefully!) quiet play.

Alternatively, clear a safe space in your home where your grandchildren can play. Make sure you have suitable chairs and a flat playing area or workspace for board games, puzzles and card games, or for activities such as writing and reading.

(**Rules** for many indoor games, such as cards and board games, have been handed down from family to family. If you find that some of the rules in this book are slightly different from the ones you usually follow, stick with the ones you know.)

 Tips

In order to keep everyone safe, you need to have some basic rules, such as:

- No running or jumping inside!
- No throwing balls inside!

Board games

Young children enjoy playing traditional, old-fashioned board games such as snakes and ladders or Monopoly. Today, many traditional games have been given a new twist and provide a challenge for older kids – and grandparents. Ask your grandchildren to bring their favourite games with them when they visit, and also keep a supply of board games in your cupboard.

Age level: All ages

What you need: Any board game

Number of players: 2 or more

How to play:
- Explain the game's structure and rules carefully.
- Players must agree on the rules for each game – and follow them.
- Simplify or change the rules for younger grandchildren.
- Keep the action moving as this can prevent disagreements.
- End the game when the interest is high.
- Make sure you pack games away carefully. Store them in a safe place.

Scoring

Playing games should be a cooperative, rather than a competitive event. Scoring is a way of encouraging each player to play well, but it should never be used to prove that one player is better than another. If scoring becomes more important than playing, abandon the game for another time.

 Grandparent tip
- Garage sales and charity shops are great places to find board games at bargain prices.

Block dominoes

Age level: 5–8 years

Number of players: 2

What you need: A set of dominoes – 28 pieces
Dominoes is a very old game from China and many different versions are played all around the world. Block dominoes is one of the simplest.

How to play:
- Place all the dominoes face down and mix them around well.
- Each player takes 7 pieces.
- The remaining domino pieces are left face down in the centre.
- The player with the highest domino plays first.
- The next player matches the domino by adding to either side. Domino pieces with different sections of dots are placed end to end; pieces with double sections of dots are placed at right angles to the line of play.

- If a player is unable to match their domino, they have to pick up another one from the table.
- The winner is the player who gets rid of all their domino pieces first or has the least number of dots on their dominoes when no more moves can be made.

Scoring

The winner of each game scores the number of dots on their opponent's pieces. The totals are tallied and the first player to reach 100 wins.

Grandparent tip

- Very young players can play with dominoes up to the number 5 or dominoes with pictures on them instead of numbers. There is no need to score as the game is more about matching and fun at this level.

Jigsaw puzzles

A jigsaw puzzle can be a satisfying problem-solving activity for grandchildren.

Age level: 3–12 years

Number of players: 1 or more

What you need:

- ▣ A jigsaw puzzle appropriate to your grandchildren's problem-solving skills – choose one with many small pieces for older children, and a puzzle with fewer, larger pieces for smaller children.
- ▣ A large piece of cardboard or a firm surface to work on. A moveable firm surface such as strong cardboard allows the puzzle to be moved while it is in various stages of completion.

How to play:

- ◎ Spread the jigsaw pieces out onto a firm surface, coloured side up.
- ◎ Find all four-corner pieces and lay them in the appropriate corner on the board.
- ◎ Group all the straight edges together and then group the rest of the pieces by colour.
- ◎ Put the puzzle together piece by piece.

◉ Grandparent tips

- Garage sales and school fêtes are good places to find jigsaw puzzles at bargain prices – although there could be a few pieces missing.
- Store and label jigsaw puzzles in ziplock bags in their boxes to avoid losing pieces.

Make your own jigsaw puzzles

Grandchildren can use drawings, paintings or family photographs to make their own special jigsaw puzzles.

Age level: 3–12 years

Number of players: 1 or more

What you need:

- A colourful picture from an old calendar or magazine, a photo, or art supplies to paint your own picture.
- A piece of cardboard.
- Glue.
- Paintbrush.
- Clear acrylic paint.
- Scissors.

What to do:

- Glue the picture onto the cardboard.
- When it is dry, paint the puzzle with clear acrylic paint to protect it.
- When the puzzle is dry, cut it into small pieces. The more pieces there are, the harder it will be to put together.
- Now the puzzle is ready to be solved.

Grandparent tips

- Copies of large family photos make fascinating puzzles for grandchildren.
- Grandchildren can make cards or write letters, then cut them into puzzle pieces and send them to their friends.

Card games

A pack of playing cards can provide hours of entertainment for grandchildren of all ages. Card games are also great learning tools. Start with simple card games and move on to more complex games as your grandchildren's skills develop.

Snap

Most grandparents will remember playing this fun card game as a child. Your grandchildren will enjoy it, too.

Age level: 5–8 years

Number of players: 2 or more

What you need:

- 1 pack of cards.
- 2 packs for 4 or more players.

How to play:

- Each player is dealt an equal number of cards, face down, until the whole pack has been dealt. Players should keep their cards face down in a pile in front of them.
- To start, each player turns over the top card from their pile and places it in the middle of the players. If the cards are not the same, one player after another turns over a second card, then a third card etc, until matching cards turn up.
- The first player to notice the matching cards says, 'Snap!' and wins all the cards that have been turned up so far. The player collects them all these cards and places them face down at the bottom of their pile.
- Play continues until a player 'snaps' all of their opponent's cards.

Animals

A delightfully noisy game and a close relative to Snap

Age level: 5–8 years

Number of players: 2 or more

What you need:
- 1 pack of cards.
- 2 packs for 4 or more players.

How to play:
- Each player chooses an animal and their accompanying noise (for example, meow for a cat, woof for a dog, moo for a cow, cock-a-doodle-doo for a rooster, hiss for a snake, quack for a duck).
- Each player is dealt an equal number of cards, face down, until the whole pack has been dealt.
- To start, each player turns over the top card from their pile and places it in the middle of the players.
- When a player turns over a card that matches one already turned up, the first person to call out the animal noise of that player wins the stack.
- The winner is the player with all or most of the cards.

Match the cards

This game tests the memory of grandchildren and grandparents alike! The idea is to remember where certain cards are, and to pair them with matching cards.

Age level: all ages

Number of players: 2–6

What you need:

- 1 pack of cards.

How to play:

- Place all the cards face down on a table or on the floor.
- The first player turns over any two cards. If they make a pair of matching cards (for example, two aces), the player picks them up. If they don't make a pair, the cards are placed face down again, and it is the next player's turn.
- The winner is the player with the most pairs.

Fish

The aim of this game is to collect four-of-a-kind sets of cards (for example, four kings, four fives).

Age level: 5–8 years

Number of players: 2–5

What you need:

▨ 1 pack of cards.

How to play:

◎ Each player is dealt five cards.

◎ The remaining cards are placed face down to make a 'fish pond' in the middle.

◎ The player on the left of the dealer starts by asking the next player clockwise for a card. For example, if they have a pair of fives, that player would ask for a five.

◎ If the next player has a five they must hand it over. If not, the player says, 'fish'.

◎ The first player then has to pick up a card from the 'fish pond' and add it to their hand.

◎ If this card is the one they wanted, the player says, 'I fished upon my wish,' and can ask for yet another card from the same player. If the card is not the one they wanted, play moves to the next player who takes their turn.

◎ When a 'set' of four cards is completed, the player shows them and puts them face down in front of them. This also ends that player's turn.

◎ The winner is the first player to place all their cards down in sets of four on the table.

◎ As this is difficult to achieve, the winner is usually the player with most sets of four in front of them when the 'fish pond' is empty.

Clock patience

Clock patience is a variation of patience that will be familiar to many grandparents. It is an excellent game to teach grandchildren, who can then enjoy many hours of solo fun.

Age level: 8–12 years

Number of players: 1

What you need:

☞ 1 pack of cards, jokers removed.

How to play:

⚙ Deal twelve cards face down in a circle to represent the position of the numbers on a clock face (see diagram), then place a card in the centre face down.

⚙ Keep dealing three more rounds, placing a card in the centre of the circle after each round has been dealt.

⚙ Take one card from the centre pile of four cards and place it where it belongs on the clock face (for example, aces are 1 o'clock, jacks go to 11 o'clock, queens are 12 o'clock and kings are in the centre pile).

⚙ Take the top card from the pile you just placed one on top of and continue. If you pick a king from the centre pile, leave it there.

⚙ You are the winner if there are four kings in the centre and you have no more cards to place on the clock, i.e. all the cards are in the right spot.

♀ Grandparent tip

- Clock patience is a game of chance, so it's important that grandchildren don't feel defeated if they don't often win – it just doesn't work out sometimes.

Card houses

With patience and a pack of cards, grandchildren can build incredible houses.

Age level: 5–12 years

Number of players: 1

What you need:

- 1 pack of cards.
- A flat surface in a draught-free place where no-one will disturb the card-house builder.

How to play:

- Begin with a simple structure of four cards in a box shape.
- You will need to carefully balance the cards against each other. (Place the cards lengthwise on the ground, overlapping slightly). It will take patience and a steady hand to make them stay upright!
- Next add a roof by placing a card flat on top of the box.
- Keep working upwards and outwards, adding more and more cards to create larger and taller constructions.
- You can also make a triangle with two cards with their shortest edges touching. Make a few of these in a row, then place cards flat on top, or combine both techniques. Continue up and out!

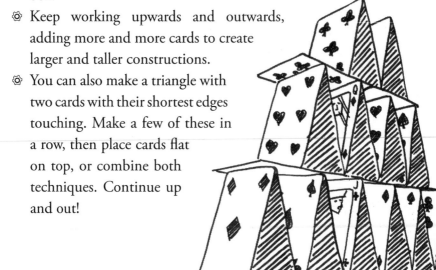

Indoor treasure hunt

Age level: 5–8 years

Number of players: 1 or more

What you need:

- Treasure – a small, easily hidden object such as a book, toy or jewellery.
- A pen or pencil.
- 'Post-it' notes or small slips of paper.

Prepare an indoor treasure hunt by providing clues for your grandchildren to find and follow. The secret to success is to prepare the hunt in advance.

What to do:

- Find a good place to hide the treasure.
- Write a series of clues, each clue leading to the next. (For example, the clue 'Look behind grandpa's favourite chair' leads you to the next clue, and so on.)
- The last clue leads to the treasure.

Treasure hunt hints

- Leave 1 clue unhidden to start the hunt.
- Hide each clue so that a small amount of paper shows.
- Don't hide clues too close together.
- A hunt for five or six good clues will last for about half an hour.
- The more rooms you use, the longer and harder the hunt will be.
- Write clues to match your grandchildren's reading ability. The best clues are those that are neither too hard nor too easy.

Grandparent tip

- Grandparent supervision will prevent small hurricanes whizzing through the house.

Magazine search

Age level: 5–12 years

Number of players: 1 or more

What you need:

▧ Pencil and paper to make a list.

▧ Old magazines and catalogues.

▧ Scissors.

A magazine hunt is an excellent indoor activity for a rainy day. Keep a stack of old magazines on-hand.

What to do:

◎ Make a list of at least 20 things, animals or people to look for in magazines.

◎ Grandparents can make lists beforehand or grandchildren can take turns adding things to the list (for example, an insect, a car, a dog, a cake or something green).

◎ Place the magazines in a pile. Hunters can only cut out one picture from a magazine at a time and then replace it in the centre for another hunter to use.

◎ Set a time limit for grandchildren to find and cut out as many different pictures on the list as possible.

◎ The winner has cut out the most pictures from the list.

♀ Grandparent tip

- Save leftover magazine pictures for another rainy day. Grandchildren can make scrapbooks, or they can write jokes, riddles or poems to fit the pictures they cut out from the magazines.

Collecting

Age level: 5–12 years

What to collect:

- Autographs.
- Erasers.
- Stamps.
- Stickers and labels.
- Rocks.
- Badges.
- Dolls.
- Miniature cars.
- Shells.
- Beads.
- Coins.
- Keys.
- Postcards.
- Sports cards.
- Books.
- Records.
- Penguins, frogs, elephants, owls ...

Some children naturally become collectors from a very early age. If you are a collector, why not share the pleasure you gain from your collection(s) with your grandchildren? By helping them to begin their own collection, you'll be starting a lifelong interest for them. You could also get them started by giving them one or two items from your own collection.

Collecting hints

- Explain that swapping or trading is necessary to add to and improve a collection.
- Steer grandchildren away from expensive collectables or those that are too hard to swap.
- Always keep in mind the golden rules:
  - Collectors never have to make a swap unless they want to.
  - Only make a swap when you have a multiple of identical objects.

Grandparent tip
- Suggest ways grandchildren can organise their collections (for example, by using albums or containers).

Codes and ciphers

Secret codes and ciphers have been around for hundreds of years. Your grandchildren will be intrigued as they learn to problem-solve their way to writing, reading and exchanging secret messages with you, their family and friends.

Alphabet code

Age level: 5–8 years

Number of players: 1 or more

What you need:

☑ Pens or pencils.

☑ Paper.

What to do:

❂ An alphabet code uses the letters of the alphabet in a different order.

❂ Write out your code with the alphabet running in the right order above, and the code below.

❂ Turn your message into code for your partner to decipher.

❂ For example, if your code was A=B, B=C, C=D etc, the word for CAT would be DBU.

❂ You can run the alphabet one way above and the other on the line below or look online for other suggestions.

Morse code and semaphore

Age level: 8–12 years

Grandparents who know morse code and/or semaphore can teach them to puzzle-loving grandchildren.

Space and backwards cipher

Age level: 8–12 years

What you need:

☞ Pens or pencils.

☞ Paper.

Writing a space and backwards cipher is quite tricky, but it's lots of fun for grandchildren.

What to do:

◎ Take out the spaces between words, for example:

AFTERNOONTEAWILLBESERVEDATTWOOCLOCK

◎ Write the message backwards:

KCOCLOOWTTADEVRESEBLLIWAETNOONRETFA

◎ Break up the message by inserting spaces between groups of 3, 4 or 5 letters:

KCOCL OOWTT ADEVR ESEBL LIWAE TNOON RETFA

◎ The deciphered message reads:

Afternoon tea will be served at two o clock.

Picket–fence code

Age level: 8–12 years

What you need:

✐ Pens or pencils.

✐ Paper.

A picket-fence code is challenging to write – and decipher!

What to do:

✪ Count the number of letters in a message. If the number cannot be divided by 2, add a dummy letter to the end of the message.

✪ Write the message, 'We will go to the beach after lunch' on two lines, with every other letter on a lower line. Do not leave any extra space between words. The message will look like the top of a picket fence:

✪ Write down the top line of letters, followed by the bottom line.

WWLGTTEECATRUCEILOOHBAHFELNH

✪ Break up the message by inserting spaces between groups of 3, 4 or 6 letters:

WWLG TTEE CATR UCEI LOOH BAHF ELNH

How to decipher a picket-fence code

⚓ Divide the message in half exactly:

WWLG TTEE CATR UC   E I LOOH BAHFE LNH

⚓ Take the first letter of the left half and follow it with first letter of the right half (for example, WE).

⚓ Next comes the second letter of the left half, followed by the second letter of the right half.

⚓ Continue until all the letters are in order.

⚓ Ignore the dummy letter, if used.

⚓ The deciphered message reads: We will go to the beach after lunch.

Cracking cipher codes

Age level: 8–12 years

What you need:
- Pens or pencils.
- Paper.

When cracking a cipher, the most important thing to remember is how often particular letters and words are likely to show up in a message.

- E is the most common letter used in the English language. T is the second most common letter used. Therefore, if one letter shows up frequently in the message, it is often an E or a T. Also note, T is the most common first letter of a word while E is the most common last letter of a word.
- The most frequently used letters in the alphabet, in order of frequency, are:
  E T A O N R I S H D L F C M U G Y P W B V K X J Q Z.
- The most frequently used words in the English language are:
  THE, OF, AND, TO, IN, IS, THAT, FOR and IT.
- If there is a single-letter word in a message, it is probably A or I. Sometimes, it might be O.
- Q is nearly always followed by U.
- The most common double letters are LL, EE, OO, TT and FF.
- TH is most often used at the beginning of a word.
- ER is most often used at the end of a word.
- The most common groups of three letters are
  THE, ING, AND, ION and ENT.

◉ Grandparent tip
- Don't use punctuation marks when writing codes or ciphers.

Secret messages

Secret messages using invisible ink are fun to exchange between grandchildren and grandparents. A secret message needs to be folded neatly and passed by hand, or left in a secret letterbox.

Age level: 8–12 years

What you need:

- 1 lemon.
- A knife.
- A bowl.
- Cotton buds.
- Paper.
- An iron.

What to do:

- Cut the lemon in half. Squeeze the juice from both halves into a bowl.
- Dip a cotton bud in lemon juice and write a message on a piece of paper.
- The message will show up when the piece of paper is pressed with a hot iron.
- The message can also be read if you dip the piece of paper in water.

> ## Grandparent tip
> - Grandparents will need to supervise their grandchildren when using an iron to decode the message.

Indoor cubby houses

Temporary, indoor cubbies provide fun spaces where grandchildren can play indoors.

Age level: 3–5 years

What you need:

- Cubbies can be made from a range of materials, including soft furnishings, chairs, stools and large boxes.
- Old sheets, towels, duvets.
- Pegs can come in handy to attach the sheets.
- Teddies, tea set or other 'essentials' for inside the cubby.
- Camping lights on headbands can be fun, too, especially at night.

Caves, castles or tents: Find a space indoors where grandchildren can build themselves a temporary cubby. Squishy cushions and old rugs and sheets can be transformed into castles, tents, caves and secret places by budding builders.

Container cubbies: The large boxes that home appliances are transported in make excellent indoor cubby houses. They're big enough to have doors and windows cut into them, and they can be painted and decorated, inside and out, though preferably outdoors (see Outdoor Games and Activities).

Designer cubbies: Grandparents who can sew can make a designer cubby out of strong material that will fit over the dining table or a card table. Simply sew four walls onto an old tablecloth, then cut out a door and several windows. The walls can be decorated with fabric paint. You'll find this cubby is an excellent game to have folded away in a cupboard for indoor play on a wet day. (See Google images, Pinterest or crafty websites for more ideas.)

Quick cubbies and hideaways: If you're in a hurry, or need a cubby quickly, drape an old bedspread or rug over a table. Alternatively, you can cover a playpen with rugs or bedspreads. Just make sure it is sturdy, and won't topple over.

Dressing up

Children love to play dress-ups. It provides a wonderful escape into the world of make-believe. When you have put together a collection of dress-ups, you'll find that older grandchildren will enjoy borrowing from your collection for school performances, plays and parties, too.

Age level: 3–12 years

What to collect:
- Capes, cloaks and coats.
- Hats, uniform caps, crowns and berets.
- Shawls, scarves and gloves.
- Wigs and waistcoats.
- Shoes (high heels are very popular with young granddaughters but they can be dangerous).
- Evening clothes.
- Jewellery – beads, earrings, feathers, tiaras.
- Handbags, belts, bow ties and braces.
- Old curtains.

What to do:
- Search your wardrobe. That once-loved hat could provide a jumping-off point into the land of make-believe for children.
- Ask friends and relatives for donations of suitable clothing for dress-ups.
- Hunt around pre-loved shops for old clothes and props.
- Disinfect and wash clothes well.
- Have a full-length mirror nearby.
- Make sure clothes and props can be put on easily and worn safely. You may need to shorten hems and sleeves and add velcro in place of complicated fasteners for young grandchildren.
- Grandparents who enjoy sewing will be able to create great dress-ups such as fairy or pirate gear.

💡 Grandparent tip

- Store dress-ups in a large, strong cardboard box. Your grandchildren can then paint and decorate the box.

Performing plays and talent shows

Children love to entertain, dress up and perform. Why not set up a space where you can join in dressing up, singing, acting and performing karaoke with your grandchildren?

Putting on a talent show

A talent show is a fun event to hold when your grandchildren visit. Grandparents can also help grandchildren to prepare a talent show to stage at home for their parents and friends.

Age level: 5–12 years

What you need:

- Friends and family members. When not performing, they can sit in the audience and clap loudly at the end of each act. Pets, dolls, bears and other toys can substitute when talent acts and audience members are unavailable.
- Helpers to sell tickets, show people to their seats, prepare refreshments for interval and introduce the acts.

What to do:

- Make a date and/or time for the talent show. Ensure participants have enough time to rehearse their act and plan their performance.
- Organise the number and order of acts.
- Make programmes, tickets and advertising material.
- Find a safe place to perform, either by clearing a space indoors or by creating a space in the garden.
- Prepare lighting, music, costumes and props.
- Provide seating for the audience.
- Make refreshments to serve at interval.

Suggested acts:

- 👍 Reading or reciting a poem.
- 👍 Doing a dance.
- 👍 Singing.
- 👍 Telling jokes.
- 👍 Acting a charade.
- 👍 Performing a small play about something that happened at school or home.
- 👍 Karaoke, miming or singing aloud to music.
- 👍 Performing acrobatics.
- 👍 Juggling.
- 👍 A pet act.
- 👍 In fact, anything the performer wants to do!

Putting on a play

Many famous actors, directors and producers have begun their careers in very, very amateur productions. Grandparents can help inspire grandchildren to perform.

Age level: 8–12 years

What you need:

- A script or a play to perform.
- Actors, props or costumes.
- An audience.

What to do:

- Help your grandchildren write a play to perform. Let their imagination take wings. Help them decide what the characters will say and do.
- If actors are scarce, toys and pets can substitute. Grandparents and grandchildren can play multiple roles or dub voices from offstage.
- Find appropriate props and costumes. You can start by searching through the dress-up box.
- Design and make tickets, programmes and posters.
- Hold a full dress rehearsal.
- Hold an opening night or matinee for family and friends.

> ## Grandparent tip
> - Putting on a play requires lots of rehearsals – an excellent time-filling activity on dull or rainy days.

Building a stage

You can erect a 'proscenium arch' in the garden, on the veranda or in a doorway to make a stage where your grandchildren can perform. Explain to your grandchildren that a proscenium arch is the shape that has been used in theatres for hundreds of years and is still used in modern theatres.

Age level: 8–12 years

What you need:

- ✒ 3 pieces of strong cardboard 2.5 m long by 60 cm wide. If you don't have long lengths of cardboard, you could glue smaller pieces together.
- ✒ Paint.
- ✒ Paintbrushes.
- ✒ Strong glue or sticky tape.

What to do:

- ✣ Label the back of the pieces of cardboard with the numbers 1, 2, 3.
- ✣ Places the pieces of cardboard on the ground outside and paint the front of them.
- ✣ Let the pieces dry.
- ✣ When piece number 2 is dry, write the name of your theatre on it.
- ✣ When part 2 is dry again, join part 1 to part 2 with glue or sticky tape.
- ✣ Then join part 3 to part 2, to form an arch.
- ✣ Lean your stage against a doorway or tie it between a couple of trees in the garden.

A stage curtain

Age level: 8–12 years

What you need:

- A large piece of material the size of the opening of the arch.
- Tacks or small nails and a hammer.
- A hook.
- Cord or wide ribbon.
- A chair for the stagehand at the side of the stage.
- A temporary stage curtain adds atmosphere to any performance. A stagehand can be waiting at the side of the stage to tie back the curtain.

What to do:

- Tack a large piece of material along the inside of the arch with a hammer.
- Secure the hook and cord or ribbon so that the curtain can be tied when it is pulled back.

Charades

Playing charades has entertained many generations of families and is lots of fun. A player acts out a secret word, book, film title or TV programme. Other players have to guess the answer.

Age level: 8–12 years

Number of players: 4 or more players (players are divided into 2 teams)

How to play:

- Team A thinks of a word or words with two or more syllables (for example, 'movie star').
- A player from Team A acts out each word. If a word is made up of a number of syllables, each syllable can be acted out separately.
- The player holds up the number of fingers to equal the number of syllables or words to be guessed. The place of each word in the answer is shown by holding up the corresponding number of fingers.
- A long word is indicated by stretching out your hands.
- A short word is indicated by holding your hands closer together.
- 'Sounds like' can be shown by pulling your ear and miming the word.
- Plural words are indicated by two fingers hooked together.
- When a player from Team B calls out the right answer for a syllable or word, the Team A player puts a hand on their nose and points with the other hand to the player to let them know they have guessed correctly.
- Team B has three guesses or a time limit to guess the whole word.
- Then it's Team B's turn to act or mime.

Music-making

Dancing, singing and making music are a magical blend for children. Musical grandparents will already know how to impart their love of music to their grandchildren but even those who swear they don't know their left foot from their right, can't sing a note or play a tin whistle can still have loads of fun sharing musical activities with their grandchildren.

Age level: 3–12 years

Number of players: any

What you need:

- Musical instruments you may have around the home or can borrow. Toy libraries often have musical instruments, microphones and other musical props you can borrow.
- Toy musical instruments.
- Anything that can make a sound – from an ice-cream container and wooden spoon to rice in a Tupperware container.
- Borrow tapes, CDs and DVDs from your local library.

Hints for 'unmusical' grandparents

There is no need to play an instrument to entertain grandchildren. Music is all around us and very easy to access for grandchildren.

- Sing nursery rhymes and teach songs from your childhood to very young grandchildren.
- If you really have no pitch, older grandchildren will soon let you know!
- You can play CDs or listen to your grandchildren playing instruments or singing.
- Whichever type of music you enjoy – classical, jazz, rock and roll, pop or folk – share your enjoyment with your grandchildren.
- Listen to different types of music. Tune into your older grandchildren's favourite music.
- Explore the power of a microphone – a toy prop or a karaoke game can give confidence to performers, young and old!

Dancing

Dancing is a delightful outlet for grandparents and grandchildren alike, livening up the dullest day!

Create your own dance floor!

Explore all forms of dance – especially the dances you know or new ones you would like to learn: jazz, ballet, tap, modern, folk, square dancing, ballroom, the twist or rock and roll.

Age level: 3–12 years

Number of children: any

What you need:

- A big open space or take your dancing outdoors!
- CD or DVD player and music or DVDs.

What to do:

- Clear a space.
- Find some toe-tapping music and turn it up!
- Jiggle, wiggle, tap, arabesque, slither and slide around the room with your grandchildren.
- Direct your grandchildren from the sideline as they dance.
- Videotapes or DVDs that demonstrate steps are fun to share with older grandchildren. Just turn on the music and practise!

Grandparent tip

- Grandparents can tutor older grandchildren when they need to learn dance steps for school dances.

Streamer dancing

Grandchildren will enjoy using colourful streamers as dancing props. Keep them in the cupboard for when dancing grandchildren visit.

Age level: 3–8 years

Number of children: any

What you need:

- Colourful wide ribbons or crepe paper.
- CD or DVD player and music or DVDs.
- A piece of dowel or similar, about 30 cm long.
- Sticky tape.

What to do:

- Cut the ribbons or streamers into 2 m lengths.
- Start with one ribbon. Explore the ways the ribbon can make designs in the air.
- Make designs above your head and close to the floor.
- Make up-and-down movements.
- Make a figure eight, first small and then large.
- Stretch out your arms to the side and make big and small circles.
- Now try these movements with two ribbons, one in each hand.
- Next, move from place to place, taking the ribbons with you.
- Try skipping, running and walking.
- Find some music that blends with your grandchildren's streamer dances. If you can't find any music, you can all sing or hum a tune.
- If you like, you can attach the streamers to a piece of dowel with some sticky tape and see what happens when you dance with the ribbon.
- Find videos of ribbon dancing on YouTube, it really is amazing!

Aerobic dancing

Age level: 5–12 years

Number of children: 1 or more

What you need:
✒ CD or DVD player and music or DVDs.

Aerobic dancing is energetic and enjoyable, and will certainly keep grandchildren and grandparents fit.

What to do:
◎ Choose music that has a good clear beat, is rhythmic and lasts for about 20 minutes.

◎ Think up an assortment of dance moves that you can join together into a sequence. For example, you could jog in one place, then jump forwards and backwards, hop on one foot and then the other, then make star jumps (a jump with legs together, followed by a jump with legs apart).

◎ Write the movements down so you can remember them.

◎ Practise and repeat.

♀ Grandparent tips
- Aerobic activity increases the oxygen supply to your heart, lungs and all your other body parts. Have fun, but try not to overdo it at the beginning.
- Watch aerobic classes on TV and write down the steps or moves. This will add variety to your dance sessions.

Storytelling

Age level: 3–12 years

Number of children: any

What you need:
- Pens or pencils.
- Paper.

Storytelling is a centuries-old tradition and an activity that requires almost no equipment. Telling stories stretches the imagination for both the teller and the listener. Grandparents can share their storytelling skills and then switch roles with their grandchildren, becoming the listener rather than the teller.

What to do:
- Write down a few sentences to describe the beginning, middle and end of the story you're going to tell.
- Practise and polish your presentation. Practise words and facial expressions in front of the mirror. You will need to describe characters, set the scene and create lots of excitement and action to make the story come alive for your listeners.
- Maintain eye contact with your listeners. If your audience starts to get restless, increase the excitement in your story.
- Use different voices, for example, a gruff voice for baddies and a soft voice for goodies, a deep voice for bears, a squeaky voice for mice.
- Adapt traditional folk and fairy stories. Make them personal by including grandchildren's, family and friends' names and other details.
- Use props such as an enchanted ring or hat to add magic to your storytelling.
- Puppets make excellent props, and can make stories come alive for listeners.
- Grandchildren love to hear stories about their parents – uncool childhood behaviour can be especially fascinating!

🔆 Grandparent tips

- Many grandparents come from cultures with strong storytelling traditions. Recall the stories you were told as a child and pass them down to your grandchildren.
- Storytelling can be a soothing, calming activity for young listeners – and a useful time-filler in emergencies.

Books and reading

Age level: 5–12 years

Number of children: any

What you need:

✒ Your favourite books – can be picture books, novels, or non-fiction, absolutely anything that takes your interest and your grandchildren's.

Reading is one of the best activities for grandchildren and grandparents to share. Encourage your grandchildren to read for pure pleasure or relaxation by making it an enjoyable time together, and by letting them watch you relax with a book.

If you own an **e-reader** or devices such as a tablet or smart phone, you can buy **e-books** or borrow them from the library. Many favourite picture storybooks have been transformed into interactive entertainment whereby grandchildren can tap on the screen to make a dog's tail wag or swipe their fingers to turn the pages.

Some grandparents will remember a time when boys were encouraged to read action-packed books and girls were expected to read 'gentler' feminine stories. Today, there is no gender divide. **Boys and girls read across genres**, and the range and variety of books for young readers is huge.

Discover your grandchildren's reading interests and skill levels. Help them select from science fiction, adventure, fantasy, mystery, animal stories and humorous tales. Novels for older children are often grounded in reality and explore the nitty-gritty reality of families and relationships.

Read children's novels and discuss the plot and characters with your grandchildren – the good bits and the boring bits. You could even form a book club with your grandchildren – reading an agreed title in a set time and sharing what you thought of it.

Sharing the activity of reading aloud gives grandchildren a cue to the meaning of words and the flow of the story. Early readers love to share their reading ability, but watch that they don't get tired and bogged down with the effort. Sharing the reading, letting them read a page or short chapter, keeps the plot moving and continues the fun in reading.

Don't interrupt reading that is flowing to correct a **misread word**. Wait until the end of the page, or the end of the book if it is short, and then help your grandchild to recognise the correct word.

Your grandchildren will be reading for meaning, so if they read 'jumped' instead of 'hopped', for example, the meaning has been kept. They will be bringing their own experiences and knowledge to their understanding of a word.

Pause, prompt and praise is an excellent strategy to help young grandchildren who are learning to read and is often used in schools.

Pause for about eight seconds if your grandchild doesn't know a word – then prompt them by asking:

- What is the first sound of the word?
- What are other sounds in the word?
- Ask them to look at the size and shape of the word, then ask questions such as, 'What word do you think it is?', 'Does that make sense?', 'Does that look right?' and, 'Does that sound right?'

Give your grandchildren lots of praise for their efforts.

Some grandchildren are **struggling or reluctant readers**. Books that tie into popular children's films can be great choices for a grandchild who is a reluctant reader, as can books that are divided into short chapters and appeal strongly to the child's interest level. An independent children's bookseller will be able to guide you in what is likely to be appropriate for your grandchild as well as engage them.

Don't forget that you can always **share reading** – you can read a hefty number of pages, while your grandchildren can read a smaller number. And don't ignore non-fiction. Choose **information books** with exciting photographs and easily accessed text. Some grandchildren would much prefer to read a non-fiction book about space, planes or dinosaurs than a magical Harry Potter novel.

Visit your **local library**. If you aren't already a member, join up and take out library loans for your grandchildren whenever they come to visit. Chat to friendly librarians and get to know the range and variety of books that will suit your grandchildren's interests and abilities. Find out which books are 'cool' reads. Who are the popular authors? Librarians will be happy to advise you on the selection of books to suit your grandchildren's reading levels.

Talking books and CDs of books are great resources for grandparents. Your local library will have a selection to borrow, or you can buy them and build up a library in your own home. Talking books and CDs can introduce young grandchildren to books that are too difficult to read alone. As well as new stories, select favourite books you knew and loved as a child.

Books make special gifts for grandchildren. Visit a bookshop with them and select a book together or check out e-book titles online. Or if you still have a collection of **your own favourite children's books** at home, share these with your grandchildren.

⚲ Grandparent tips

- Secondhand shops, markets and online book sites are excellent places to pick up copies of children's books you loved to read as a child.
- Don't hesitate to find an easier book if your grandchild is finding the book you are reading too difficult.

Cooking

Age level: 3–12 years

Number of children: any

What you need/items to have in the pantry:

- Canned fruits, especially apricots, plums and peaches (use them for desserts as well as breakfast).
- A range of pastas and rice.
- Frozen ice cream and yoghurt.
- Tomato sauces – to go with pasta.
- Frozen peas and other vegetables.
- Fresh onions and potatoes.
- Cheese.
- Ingredients or prepared mixes to make cakes, pancakes or scones.
- A variety of spreads, for example, peanut butter, jams, jellies and preserves.
- Canned fish such as tuna and salmon.
- Tea and coffee.
- Long-life milk.
- Cocoa or chocolate drink mix.

Cooking is a great activity to do with grandchildren. It is a cool way for them to learn all sorts of things with you: maths, science, technology, reading and writing, fine motor skills, sharing, taking turns and patience. Cooking also develops your grandchildren's independence and confidence and teaches them valuable life skills – plus it's fun!

If your grandchildren have helped to make their food, they are more likely to enjoy eating it. Begin by cooking the food that your grandchildren love to eat – with their favourite smells and tastes – then introduce them to more adventurous food.

> ### ◔ Grandparent tip
> - Pass down treasured recipes to your grandchildren as they watch and cook with you.

Young grandchildren need close supervision when they use knives and other kitchen equipment. Explain your **'Kitchen Rules'** before grandchildren start cooking, for example, they must:

- Ask for your permission before cooking.
- Wash hands before they start to cook.
- Wear an apron and tie their hair back.
- Use oven cloths or potholders when handling hot containers and pots. (Only allow grandchildren to lift pots and dishes if they can do this easily and safely.)
- Grandparents need to supervise the operation of stoves and ovens of all kinds.

Very young grandchildren (3–5 years old) can help with **small jobs** such as cutting bananas for fruit salad, grating cheese, decorating cakes and desserts, podding peas and peeling carrots.

Slightly older children (6–8 years old) may need you to light the oven or they can be taught to turn it on, use a microwave oven, toaster and other kitchen equipment safely.

Children eight and over can tackle stove-top cooking and help to light the stove with constant supervision while 10-year-olds just need 'grandparent help' close by. Let them ask for help. Remind them that even top chefs need help at some time.

Encourage grandchildren to feel just as enthusiastic about **cleaning up** as cooking and eating. Even small children can do some of the following jobs.

- Put away left over ingredients and any equipment that hasn't been used.
- Wash the dishes. Start with the least dirty dishes, like glassware and bowls, and then do the messy pans and baking tins.

- Dry the dishes thoroughly and put them away.
- Stack the dishwasher if you have one. Don't forget to put the dishes away when it is finished and they are dry.
- Wipe down work surfaces with a clean cloth.
- Sweep the floor.
- Put out the rubbish.

Feeding grandchildren can be tricky. Some children have very particular likes and dislikes – and these likes and dislikes can change from day to day. Aim to keep them happy while still serving healthy food.

Allow your grandchildren to become involved with planning menus, shopping and cooking their food choices. Visit farmers' markets together so your grandchildren can get an understanding of where food comes from. Allow them to gather herbs and vegetables from your garden to use in recipes. Following are some other ideas.

- Preparing and holding a 'carpet picnic' indoors is fun on wet days – and a time-filling lifesaver. **Warning:** use plenty of protection for the carpet.
- Grandchildren can help you set an attractive table – an art that can turn the simplest meal into a celebration.
- Mastering setting and serving a simple breakfast tray (plus a flower!) will make older grandchildren popular with their families.

Caution: Grandparents need to supervise their grandchildren at all times when they are using stoves, ovens and cooking tools.

☺ Grandparent tip
- Sadly, there is little chance that a grandchild's eating patterns will change during visits with you!

Traditional pizza

Age level: 3–12 years

Number of children: any

What you need:

- A jug.
- Measuring cups and spoons.
- 2 large bowls.
- 2 oven or large, round pizza trays.

Pizza is a favourite with grandchildren – and a good excuse to get them in the kitchen!
Your grandchildren will enjoy kneading the dough when you make dough from scratch for this pizza recipe.

Note: You will need to start making this base 2½ hours before you want to eat the pizza.

Ingredients:

1 heaped tablespoon dried yeast
1 cup hot water
½ teaspoon sugar
2 tablespoons extra-virgin olive oil
400 g plain flour
1 teaspoon salt
3 tablespoons Italian-style tomato sauce
pizza toppings of choice (cheese, ham, pineapple, oregano, olives, mushroom etc.)

What to do:

- Put the yeast in a jug with the water, sugar and oil. Stir until it is dissolved. Set aside until it has risen and gone frothy.
- Place the flour and salt in a bowl.

☼ Pour in the yeast mixture and mix to make a soft ball of dough that leaves the bowl clean.

☼ Put the dough on a floured table and knead it for about 5 minutes. To knead, push the dough away from you with one hand, gather it into a ball, give it a turn and repeat.

☼ When the dough is smooth and stretchy, put it in a bowl and brush with a little olive oil. Cover it with a tea towel and place in a warm place to rise for 60–90 minutes.

☼ Preheat the oven to 230°C.

☼ When the dough has doubled in size, take it out of the bowl and knead it for 5 more minutes.

☼ Split it into two balls and place each on a lightly greased tray.

☼ Press the balls of dough out with your hands so they fill the tins. Leave it slightly raised around the edges to make a crust.

☼ Spread tomato sauce over the pizzas, leaving the edges clear.

☼ Add the toppings of your choice.

☼ Bake the pizza in the oven for 15–20 minutes until the pizza topping is soft and the dough is browned underneath.

♀ Grandparent tips

- The dough should come together in a smooth, elastic ball. If it is sticky, add a little more flour.
- Kids love putting the toppings on the pizza.

Quick pizza

This quick pizza base doesn't need kneading and you don't need to wait for the dough to rise.

Age level: 3–12 years

Number of children: any

What you need:

- ▧ 2 oven or large, round pizza trays.
- ▧ Measuring cups and spoons.
- ▧ A knife.
- ▧ A chopping board.
- ▧ A bowl.
- ▧ A rolling pin.

Ingredients:

toppings such as ham, bacon, prawns or sausage, onion, red and green capsicum, mushrooms, pitted olives, shelled peas, basil leaves or pesto
1 cup self-raising flour
¼ cup salt
4–6 tablespoons Greek-style yoghurt
1 tablespoon olive oil
minced garlic
3 tablespoons Italian-style tomato sauce
125 g grated mozzarella cheese

What to do:

- ◎ Preheat the oven to 220°C.
- ◎ Grease the pizza trays.
- ◎ Slice and dice the pizza toppings.
- ◎ Mix the flour, salt and yoghurt in bowl until a soft dough is formed.
- ◎ Roll the dough out very thinly and place on a greased pizza tray.
- ◎ Brush the dough with oil and garlic and spread the tomato sauce on top.

- Scatter half the cheese on the pizza base. Arrange the toppings on top in an attractive design.
- Top with the remaining cheese.
- Bake the pizza in the oven for 15–20 minutes until the pizza topping is soft and the dough is browned underneath.

Grandparent tip

- Pita bread or toast works well as a pizza base for hungry grandchildren. They can add their own choice of topping.

Read it, cook it and eat it!

Young grandchildren enjoy sharing traditional stories – and cooking and eating the food that stars in the stories!

For example, cook porridge when you read *The Three Bears*, make biscuits when you tell the story of *The Gingerbread Man*, and bake bread after sharing the tale of the driven *Little Red Hen*. Cook pasta after visiting the story of *The Magic Pasta Pot*. And definitely make soup after telling the clever folk tale, *Stone Soup*.

Stone soup

Age level: 3–12 years

Number of children: any

What you need:

- One very clean, magic stone (quartz is good as it is clean and won't break with boiling).
- A large saucepan with a lid.
- A large spoon.
- A knife.
- A chopping board and bread knife.
- A vegetable peeler.
- Measuring spoons and cups.
- Soup bowls.

Stone soup is an excellent way of getting young grandchildren to eat vegetables. *Stone Soup* is a traditional folk tale you can find at your library or online. A stranger visits a family and tricks them into making a delicious soup when he only contributes a stone.

Ingredients:

1 tablespoon oil

1 onion, peeled and chopped

2 litres (8 cups) vegetable stock (or use stock cubes and make the stock with boiling water)
2 tomatoes, chopped
2 carrots, peeled and sliced
1 large potato, peeled and chopped
2 celery sticks, chopped
125 g tomato paste
1 magic stone
2 zucchinis, sliced
60 g macaroni or small pasta shapes
2 tablespoons fresh parsley, chopped
fresh bread

What to do:

- ◎ Wash your magic stone in hot, slightly soapy water and then rinse.
- ◎ Heat the oil in a large pan and cook the onion until it's soft and lightly golden.
- ◎ Add the stock, tomatoes, carrots, potato, celery, tomato paste and the magic stone to the pan.
- ◎ Bring the ingredients to the boil, then reduce the heat and simmer for 1 minute.
- ◎ Add the zucchini, macaroni and parsley to the pan. Partially cover with a lid and simmer for a further 45 minutes.
- ◎ Remove the stone and serve the soup steaming hot in bowls with big chunks of fresh bread.

☺ Grandparent tip
- Alphabet pasta is fun for young grandchildren.

Magic pasta pot spaghetti and meat sauce

Spaghetti and meat sauce is an all-time favourite with grandchildren.

Age level: 3–12 years

Number of children: any

What you need:

- Wooden spoons.
- Measuring spoons and cups.
- 2 large pans (preferably with lids).
- A knife.
- A chopping board.
- A can opener.
- A colander.
- A large serving dish.

Ingredients:

1 tablespoon oil
1 onion, peeled and chopped
500 g lean minced beef
¼ teaspoon salt
¼ teaspoon pepper
1 can tomatoes, roughly chopped
125 ml (½ cup) tomato purée
1 teaspoon oregano
¼ teaspoon sugar
250 ml (1 cup) water
250 g corkscrew-shaped pasta
chopped parsley
grated cheese

What to do:

◎ Heat the oil in a large pan over a medium heat. Fry the onion until soft.

◎ Add the minced beef. Cook over medium–low heat for 5–7 minutes until the meat is no longer pink. Stir the meat occasionally with a wooden spoon so that it browns easily.

◎ Add salt, pepper, canned tomatoes, tomato purée, oregano, sugar and water. Stir well until it starts to boil.

◎ Turn the heat to low and simmer for 40 minutes or alternatively, place a lid on top and cook in a moderately slow oven.

◎ Fill a big pot with water. You need it to be about three-quarters full. Bring the water to the boil and add a little salt.

◎ Drop the pasta into the boiling, salted water.

◎ Boil the pasta for 10 minutes until it is tender. Drain well.

◎ Pour the pasta into a large serving dish, then pour the hot mince over it. Sprinkle with chopped parsley.

◎ Place in individual bowls and serve with a bowl of grated cheese.

◉ Grandparent tip

- Pasta dishes are popular with most grandchildren. They can try different kinds of pasta such as farfalle (butterflies), penne (quills or pens), fettuccine (ribbons) and vermicelli (little worms).

Gingerbread people

Age level: 3–12 years

Number of children: any

What you need:

- Gingerbread man biscuit (cookie) cutter or cardboard and scissors.
- 2 baking trays.
- Measuring spoons and cups.
- A sieve.
- A mixing bowl.
- Beaters.
- A jug.
- A fork.
- A wooden spoon.
- A rolling pin.
- Biscuit cutters.
- Baking paper.

Biscuits (cookies) can be made using a biscuit (cookie) cutter. You can also make the biscuits into any other shapes that your grandchildren would like.

☺ Grandparent tip

- If you don't have the correct biscuit cutter, simply draw the shape on a piece of clean, heavy cardboard, then cut it out. Grease the shape on one side with butter or oil and place the greased side down on the biscuit dough. Cut around the shape with a knife. Re-roll the uncut bits of dough to use for more shapes.

Ingredients:

125 g butter

1 cup brown sugar

2 cups self-raising flour

1 teaspoon cinnamon

2 teaspoons ground ginger

1 egg

currants for eyes, mouth and buttons

What to do:

◎ Preheat the oven to 180°C.

◎ Grease two baking trays or line with baking paper.

◎ In a mixing bowl, beat the butter and sugar together until light and fluffy.

◎ Sift the flour and spices together over the butter and sugar.

◎ Using your fingertips, work the butter into the mixture so it looks like breadcrumbs.

◎ Break the egg into a jug and beat with a fork.

◎ Make a hole in the flour mixture and add the beaten egg.

◎ Mix everything together until you have a firm ball of dough. Turn the dough onto a lightly floured work surface and knead gently for 1 minute.

◎ Roll the dough out with a lightly floured rolling pin to around 1 cm thick.

◎ Use a cutter to cut out the biscuits, or your grandchildren can cut around the shapes they made.

◎ Gather up any leftover dough, then roll it out again and cut out more shapes.

◎ Put the biscuits on the two trays.

◎ Place the currants on the biscuits for eyes, buttons, etc.

◎ Bake on a high shelf in the oven for 15–20 minutes, or until light brown.

◎ Put the biscuits on a wire rack to cool.

ⓠ Grandparent tips

- Recipe can also be made in a Mixmaster or food processor.
- Grandchildren can use the floured top of a glass if you haven't got a biscuit cutter.
- If you put the ball of dough in a plastic bag and place it in the refrigerator for 30 minutes, it will be easier to roll out.
- Biscuits can also be iced and decorated with lollies instead of currants.

Art and craft activities

Introduction

Providing **art and craft activities** for your grandchildren will give them the opportunity to discover, learn and practise useful skills. The simplest of activities, such as drawing with pencils or cutting-and-pasting can liven a dull, wet day for young children – with a minimum of fuss.

Art and craft **supplies** are invaluable resources when grandchildren come to stay. Include basic supplies such as:

- Paper.
- Felt-tip pens, textas, crayons, coloured pencils, watercolour pencils, paints and chalk.
- Children's scissors.
- Paste or glue.
- Sticky tape.
- A hole-punch.
- A stapler.
- Glitter, stickers, stamps etc.

A **junk box** filled with creative materials that you can bring out on rainy days or when you all need some quiet time can be helpful, too. Grandparents are excellent recyclers – they know junk can be transformed into brilliantly artistic, creative works. Your junk box could include:

- Bottle tops.
- Cardboard cylinders and packages.
- Cotton reels.
- Cotton wool.
- Wool and yarn.
- Fabric scraps.
- Chocolate wrappers.
- Paper bags and wrapping paper.
- Cellophane.
- Old gift cards.
- Old magazines.
- Confetti.
- Beads.
- Sequins.
- Buttons.
- Nuts and seeds.
- Feathers and shells.
- Dried flowers and grasses.

Caution: Always supervise young children when they use glue, scissors and sharp objects.

ℚ Grandparent tip
- Supermarkets, craft- and office-supply stores stock materials to suit all budgets. They can be treasure troves of inspiration for art and craft activities for grandchildren.

Plan activities and prepare materials and equipment well ahead of time. Consider the following:

- Smocks to protect your grandchildren's clothing, or you could give them an old shirt to wear. For particularly messy but fun activities you could cut openings for head and arms in a large plastic garden bag. Supervision at all times is essential if your grandchildren are young, especially with plastic bags.
- A table or flat working area.
- Protective covering for the working area and surrounding floor. Use plastic sheeting, such as a shower curtain, to catch messy drips and spills.

When ready, clear a space where grandchildren can safely create their own art and craft masterpieces.

🔆 Grandparent tip

- Cleaning up is an inescapable part of the creative process. Include your grandchildren as helpers, but if the going is very slow and you're feeling a little desperate, deposit small children in a safe place to watch while you quickly clean up yourself.

Drawing

Drawing is a favourite creative activity for grandchildren of all ages that can be set up anywhere, any time. Encourage your grandchildren's natural artistic talent, allowing them to express themselves in their own way.

Age level: 3–12 years

Number of children: any

What you need:
- Well-sharpened coloured or watercolour pencils.
- Felt-tip pens, textas, crayons or pastels.
- Lead pencils such as 2B or HB.
- A variety of different thicknesses of ballpoint pens.
- A variety of papers and a surface or drawing board to rest on.

Remember, there is **no right or wrong** way in art, so avoid asking too many probing questions about young artists' drawings such as, 'What is it?' or 'Where are the arms?' It's better to say, 'Tell me about your drawing.'

Most young children will not draw anything that looks like a known person, animal or object for some time. Until around four years of age, they will be experimenting with colour and their use of implements such as pencils, pens and brushes. Then, at about four years old, they will draw or paint symbols such as the sun, and they will also begin to draw themselves, then family members. Soon, other familiar symbols will come into their artwork.

You can give older grandchildren a starting point by suggesting that they draw a large shape and then fill in the details. Encourage them to experiment with varying lines – thick outlines for things that are near, light lines for things in the distance.

☺ Grandparent tip
- Drawing on the pavement or drive with chalk is a sign for neighbours that grandchildren are visiting! Colourful pavement art (which can fill hours) will fade away or can be hosed away ready for their next visit.

Drawing in the dark

Pull the blinds shut, turn off the lights and have fun drawing in the dark with your grandchildren. For young children especially, letting a pencil dance on paper is as natural as running and jumping.

Age level: 3–12 years

Number of children: any

What you need:
- Pencils.
- Paper.

What to do:
- Turn off the lights.
- You can provide ideas for what to draw, for example, a cat. Add some challenges for older grandchildren such as, 'Now draw a mouse in the cat's mouth!'
- Turn on the lights and enjoy the results!

Grandparent tips
- It pays to invest in a small supply of good-quality pencils that have strong colours, they will give the best results.
- Good-quality watercolour pencils are a very satisfactory art medium for children. They are much easier to use than watercolour paints, and artists young and old can achieve fantastic effects when they use them.

Still-life drawing

Drawing from life is a challenging art activity for older grandchildren. However, with a few helpful tips they will be able to create a masterpiece of the first order.

Age level: 8–12 years

Number of children: any

What you need:

☞ Paper.

☞ Pencils, felt-tip pens, watercolour pencils or crayons.

☞ A subject. For example, a bowl of fruit; a collection of objects such as a teapot, jug, cup and saucer; or a teddy bear and other soft toys.

What to do:

◈ Collect some objects from around the house. Set them up in an arrangement to be drawn.

◈ Discuss and demonstrate still-life drawing hints. For example, explain how to draw an object that is in front of another. The hint is to draw the object that is in front first, and to then draw the object that is behind it. When the pencil runs into the first object, jump over it and keep going on the other side.

◈ Grandchildren can sign their masterpieces. The pictures can then be hung on the walls to be admired or kept by grandparents for posterity.

Self-portrait

Age level: 5–12 years

Number of children: any

What you need:

- A mirror.
- Pencils and coloured pencils.
- A large sheet of drawing paper.

Drawing a self-portrait is an engrossing art activity for grandchildren. They can create enchanting and insightful portraits of themselves for you to keep.

What to do:

- Assist your grandchildren as they look at themselves in the mirror. Discuss the shape of their faces and the placement of their features. For example, point out that their ears are on a horizontal line with their eyes.
- Talk about the colour of your grandchildren's eyes, hair and skin.
- Be ready with plenty of praise as they complete their masterpieces.

Self-portrait drawing hints

- The face is around two-thirds as wide as it is long.
- Eyes are about halfway up the face.
- The distance from the eyebrows to the end of the nose is usually the same distance as from the end of the nose to the tip of the chin.
- The space between the eyes generally equals one eye width.

Painting

Age level: 3–12 years

Number of children: any

What you need:

- A basic set of water-based paints – red, blue, yellow, black and white. Encourage your grandchildren to mix and explore other colours from these basic colours. Ready-mixed water-based paints can be bought in economy sizes and kept in the cupboard.
- Use yoghurt pots to hold the paint if your grandchildren are young. Pack the pots firmly into a shallow cardboard box, so if they are knocked over they won't make too much mess.
- An egg carton, an old patty-cake tin or an old plate can be used as an artist's palette to mix paint.
- A collection of different-sized paintbrushes. Older grandchildren may prefer to use smaller brushes.
- Thick, absorbent paper is best for young grandchildren. Coloured paper can be used for special projects such as cards. Recycled computer paper, architect's paper and rolls of wallpaper make good paper for painting.
- Grandchildren will be happy to paint on a table, flat on the floor or at an easel, which makes painting easier for young children. You can turn a child's blackboard into an easel by covering it with plastic and using bulldog clips to attach the paper.
- Paint is a wonderfully creative medium for grandchildren to use – but it's messy! A little anti-mess protection can render painting a fun and environmentally friendly art activity.

Children often create dazzling works of art when they paint. Sometimes there will be a definite story behind their paintings. Other times they will be experimenting with lots of colour and big, broad brushstrokes. They will probably make up what it is about – just to keep you happy.

What to do

- ▤ Protective clothing is an absolute must for painting activities.
- ▤ Before your grandchildren begin painting, set aside a space to dry their wet artworks, preferably outside, or pegged onto a clothes rack to dry inside.
- ▤ Whenever possible, set up painting activities outdoors. Easels, surroundings and grandchildren can then be more easily washed down at the end of the painting session.
- ▤ Provide small quantities of each paint colour at a time and lots of paper!
- ▤ For older children, you could leave out something for them to paint, like a bowl of fruit, or make suggestions en plein air such as the magnolia tree in flower in your garden.
- ▤ Wash paintbrushes and pots well so they are ready for the next painting session.
- ▤ To keep brushes soft, wash them thoroughly and store them in plastic wrap.

Learning **different painting techniques** can provide a challenge for grandchildren. Try the following techniques:

- ▤ Blowing bubbles of thin paint onto paper with a straw (careful not to suck the paint up into your mouth).
- ▤ Using a variety of objects instead of brushes, for example, feathers, sticks, leaves, crumpled paper or pieces of sponge.
- ▤ Splatter painting – using an old toothbrush dipped in paint and brushed over a piece of flywire. Or you can literally flick the bristles to create a splatter.
- ▤ Dot painting – using a fine brush, felt-tip pen or cotton buds, make tiny dots of colour.
- ▤ Finger painting – start by spreading large dollops of paint on the paper.
- ▤ Use old toy cars to run through paint and make patterns.
- ▤ Buy a new plastic tray (such as those used for kitty litter), place a piece of paper inside and roll around some marbles or balls dipped in paint.
- ▤ Sponges cut into different shapes to use as brushes can be fun, too.

☺ Grandparent tips

- Don't be surprised if young grandchildren spend only a short time on one painting. This is quite normal. However, if your grandchild paints only one stroke and then wants a new piece of paper, encourage them to continue painting on the paper they have.
- To display your grandchildren's paintings, peg them onto wire coathangers and hang them from hooks on the wall or from the ceiling.
- If you have limited painting facilities at your home, don't worry. Your grandchildren will be exploring their creativity with paint at preschool, school or in their own home.

Printing

Printing is great fun but, like painting, it can get very messy! Protect your grandchildren and surrounding areas to ensure printing is a happy, stress-free activity.

Hand and feet prints

Printing grandchildren's hands and feet onto paper is great fun. The prints make sentimental mementoes to keep. Remember this is definitely an outdoor activity.

Age level: 3–5 years

Number of children: any

What you need:

- A tray or flat dish – big enough to fit your grandchildren's feet and hands.
- Paint.
- Paper.
- A container of water and towels to wash and dry hands and feet after these activities is essential.

What to do:

- Fill the tray or dish with paint – not too much, just enough to cover the bottom. (It is better to refill the tray than have too much paint!)
- Grandchildren can carefully place their hands or bare feet in the paint and then make a handprint or footprint on paper.
- Date the hand and feet charts and keep them for size comparisons in the years to come.

💡 Grandparent tips

- Less messy charts can be made by tracing around your grandchildren's feet while they are standing on a piece of paper. They can then fill in the shape with felt-tip pens or paint. Repeat this with your grandchildren's hands – or if you have really large paper or a roll of butcher's paper, trace around their whole body. This can also be done with chalk on concrete. (See Body-shape Posters for more ideas.)
- Pets' paw prints can also be effective. With permission from pets, grandchildren can make great decorative charts using the same process – once again, this is definitely an outdoor activity!

Fingerprint characters

Fingerprint characters are fun, easy to make – and not too messy. Protect grandchildren and surfaces before fingerprinting begins and have a damp sponge nearby for emergencies.

Age level: 5–12 years

Number of children: any

What you need:

- Paints.
- Paper.
- Felt-tip pens.
- A damp sponge.

What to do:

- Place a small dab of paint on the tip of your grandchild's finger. Spread the paint evenly.
- Press your grandchild's finger onto the paper to make a fingerprint. If the print looks too heavy, wipe off some of the paint from their finger and print again.
- Now your grandchild can let their imagination fly by adding details to their finger painting with a felt-tip pen. They can create rabbits, butterflies, flowers, trees, fish etc.

Fingerprint ideas

- Fingerprints can be used to decorate greeting cards, party invitations or stationery.
- Cluey grandchildren can take family fingerprints and use them in their detective games.
- Stamp pads can be a less-messy substitute for paint.

Leaf prints

Searching for different shapes and sizes of leaves is half the fun of this activity. You'll need to collect many leaves as they can quickly become soggy during the printing process. Older grandchildren can use this process to make cards or gift-wrapping paper.

Age level: 3–12 years

Number of children: any

What you need:
- A variety of leaves.
- Old newspapers.
- Paint.
- Paintbrushes.
- Paper.

What to do:
- Place a dry leaf on some newspaper and paint one side completely.
- Press the painted side of the leaf onto a piece of paper. Smooth it down and press it so a good print is made.
- Repeat the process. Encourage your grandchildren to experiment by overlapping the leaves. They can also use leaves to make patterns or borders.

Potato-print wrapping paper

Grandchildren will impress friends and relatives with their attractive potato-print wrapping paper. Design ideas can include stars, triangles, squares, circles and hearts.

Age level: 5–12 years

Number of children: any

What you need:
- Potatoes.
- A small knife.
- Felt-tip pens.
- Newspaper or plastic covering.
- Trays.
- Paints.
- Large sheets of paper.

What to do:
- Cover a flat working surface with newspaper or plastic covering for protection.
- Cut the potatoes in half for your grandchildren.
- Older grandchildren can draw simple designs on the potato halves with thin felt-tip pens and then cut around their design carefully with a knife to make a stamp.
- You will need to cut out the shapes for younger grandchildren. Start with simple shapes.
- Fill the trays with different coloured paints.
- Press the potato firmly in a tray of paint and then print on paper.
- Create a design to make attractive wrapping paper.
- Why not use the potato prints to make matching gift cards too?

⚲ Grandparent tips

- This activity also works well using the distinct patterns of halved fruit such as apples and lemons.
- You could also investigate other forms of printing – there are many other types appropriate to big and small children. At its simplest, you can rub paint over an area, let your grandchildren draw pictures with their fingers and then place a piece of paper over the area to make your print. Lino prints and screen-printing supplies can be found in art supply shops, and craft outlets sometimes have craft packages for different types of printing, as well as supplies.

Collages

Making a collage – cutting and pasting different materials onto a background – can keep grandchildren engaged and happy for hours. It's a relatively mess-free activity and quick to prepare, too. Just collect collage materials and keep them in a container ready to use.

Age level: 3–12 years

Number of children: any

What to collect:

- Seeds and lentils.
- Beads, sequins and buttons.
- Wool, cord, ribbon, string and lace.
- Coloured paper and old greeting cards.
- Glitter and stickers.
- Tissue paper and cellophane.

What to do:

- Newspaper and old telephone books make excellent collage materials when they are cut or torn into shapes and pasted onto a black background.
- Cut coloured paper into geometric shapes so grandchildren can make challenging mathematical collages.
- Older grandchildren can use images and photos from magazines and newspapers to make collages. For example, they can cut out eyes, ears, lips, hands, glasses, shoes or parts of animal bodies, or use patterns to represent hair, fabric or background.
- Overlapping tissue or cellophane paper can create new colours and brilliant collages when they are pasted onto black backgrounds.
- Mosaic collages can be made by drawing the outline of a picture on a white background. Grandchildren can choose coloured paper from magazines and cut or tear them into small pieces to create their mosaic collages.

♀ Grandparent tips

- Store beads, sequins, buttons etc safely in small boxes with lids.
- Protective covering for grandchildren and surfaces is essential when making collages.

Collage picture

Grandchildren can use a collection of materials of different sizes and shapes to create a collage picture.

Age level: 5–12 years

Number of children: any

What you need:
- Collage materials (see above for ideas).
- Scissors.
- Felt-tip pens.
- PVA glue.
- Sheets of paper or cardboard for background.

What to do:
- Sort collage materials into various colours and sizes. Smaller pieces of paper and fabric are easier to manage.
- Talk about the ways your grandchildren can arrange the materials and create a picture before they apply glue and finally place their collage materials.
- Your grandchildren may prefer to draw outlines such as trees and a bird before they begin their collage.

Collage gift cards

Grandchildren can use collage materials to make cards for special occasions.

Age level: 5–12 years

Number of children: 1 or more

What you need:

- Stiff card measuring 24 cm x 15 cm.
- Collage materials.
- Scrap paper.
- Glue.
- Felt-tip pens.

What to do:

- Fold the piece of card in half.
- Grandchildren can dream up a design for their card. What will be on the cover? What will be on the inside?
- They can then draw a design on the front cover and add collage materials. When the gift cards are finished, they can write a message inside.

Seed picture

A collection of seeds and lentils will provide grandchildren with easy-to-handle materials to make an unusual collage.

Age level: 5–12 years

Number of children: any

What you need:
- Background paper or card.
- Pens and pencils.
- Strong glue.
- Paint or craft brush.
- Collection of seeds, rice, wheat, beans, small-sized pasta and different coloured lentils.

What to do:
- Allow your grandchildren to experiment and explore the different shapes, sizes, textures and colours of the seeds, pasta and lentils.
- Will they create a scene, an animal, a person – or even a dinosaur? Once your grandchildren have decided on the subject of their collage picture, they can draw an outline on their background paper.
- The next step is to spread glue on parts of the picture and sprinkle seeds or lentils on top. Then push them into place with the hard end of the brush.
- Continue sticking on seeds until the picture is finished. Use contrasting pieces to create details like eyes.

Dried-flower cards

Many grandparents will remember pressing flowers when they were children. This is a two-step activity. First, press the flowers to allow them to dry, and then make the cards. Experiment with different flowers – small flowers such as daisies and violets work well.

Age level: 3–12 years

Number of children: any

What you need:

- Small flowers and leaves from the garden.
- Sheets of kitchen paper towel.
- A flower press or phone book.
- A heavy weight such as books or a brick.
- Card.
- Ribbons.
- Glue.
- Coloured pencils or felt-tip pens.

What to do:

- To press the flowers, place both the flowers and the leaves between two pieces of kitchen paper towel. Arrange the flowers so that all the petals can be seen.
- Place them in the flower press or at 20-page intervals in a phone book.
- Secure the flower press with the screws or weight the phone book with heavy books or a brick.
- Depending on the plants, the flowers will take several weeks to dry. After the flowers are pressed and dried, your grandchildren can make the cards on another visit.
- To make the card, your grandchildren will first need to decide how it will look. Is it going to be a vertical or horizontal card? Now fold it in half appropriately.

◎ Place the dried flowers and leaves in a design on the front. Bits of ribbon can be added, too.

◎ When your grandchildren are happy with their arrangement they can glue it down.

◎ Help young grandchildren with their writing to complete the card.

⚘ Grandparent tip

- Encourage grandchildren to conserve the environment and leave wildflowers where they find them.

Paper chains

Paper chains make excellent decorations for special occasions. Grand-children of all ages can join in this activity.

Age level: 3–12 years

Number of children: any

What you need:
- Strips of paper.
- Glue or a stapler and staples.
- Pins to hang up the paper chains.

What to do:
- Cut each strip of paper into 20 cm lengths.
- Take the first strip of paper and fold it over to form a loop. Glue or staple the strip together.
- Put another strip of paper through the loop and glue or staple it.
- Continue until the chain is as long as you need.
- Hang the chain up and enjoy your hard work.

Tips for using staplers

Take young grandchildren through the steps needed to use a stapler.
1   Place a stapler flat on the table.
2   Press the stapler hard with both hands until they hear two clicks.
3   Practise and be patient.

People paper-chains

Many grandparents will remember making paper-chain dolls on a rainy day. Today, grandchildren will have just as much fun making paper people.

Age level: 5–12 years

Number of children: 1 or more

What you need:

- Paper cut into strips measuring about 10 cm x 22 cm.
- Pencils, coloured pencils, felt-tip pens.
- Scissors.

What to do:

- Fold the paper using a zigzag or accordion fold about 5 cm wide. Make sure you don't use too many folds because it will be too thick to cut!
- Draw a simple figure on the top fold. The figure must touch both sides of the paper to make a chain.
- Cut around your figure, but not where it touches the sides.
- Unfold the paper chain to reveal the row of figures linked by their hands and feet.
- Colour and decorate your chain of people.
- Hang up your paper chains. You could also join them to make party hats or frills around cakes.

Grandparent tips

- Older grandchildren can use a ruler to mark out lengths of paper about 5 cm wide.
- Chains of large paper people, stars, animals and other shapes are fun to make. They are excellent party decorations for older grandchildren's parties.

Constructions

Age level: 3–8 years

Number of children: any

What to collect:

- Cardboard boxes of all shapes and sizes.
- Cardboard rolls.
- Corrugated card.
- Aluminium foil.
- Plastic bottle tops.
- Plastic food containers.

A collection of cardboard boxes and recycled materials provide endless fun for young grandchildren. Sealed, empty boxes make great construction blocks. Your grandchildren can also decorate a large carton to use as a toy box at your house.

Pull-along cart

Very young grandchildren will love to make a pull-along cart to use indoors. The cart can carry mysterious loads or their teddy.

Age level: 3–5 years

Number of children: any

What you need:

- A large carton.
- Thick cord or rope.
- Pencils, felt-tip pens and coloured paper for decoration.
- Scissors.
- Paste or glue.

What to do:

- Grandparents will need to make two holes in one side of the carton to insert a pull-along cord handle.
- The cart can be used as it is, or your grandchildren can decorate it with felt-tip pens and paint or glue on cut-out shapes.
- Store the cart in a cupboard or the shed so your grandchildren can play with it when they visit.

3-D model

Grandparents don't need to provide expensive materials or kits for grandchildren to make exciting 3-D models. A collection of recycled materials, plus a grandparent to help hold, glue and fasten models, is a perfect combination.

Age level: 3–5 years

Number of children: any

What you need:
- Cartons and boxes of all sizes.
- Lids and bottle tops.
- PVA glue.
- Scissors.
- Paint and paintbrush.
- Felt-tip pens.

What to do:
- Talk about the kinds of model your grandchildren can construct. Will it be a castle, a car, a robot or an animal? The recycled materials will inspire ideas and the children can experiment with the materials to arrange their own construction.
- Glue together the basic structure. Arms, legs and features can be added to the body and head of a robot, feet and ears to an animal, bonnet and wheels to a car.
- The model can be painted.
- When the model is dry, details such as handles on doors and whiskers on faces can be painted or stuck on.

Grandparent tips
- Protect grandchildren with aprons or smocks, and cover tables and floor areas with newspaper or plastic.
- Organise a space for constructions to be left to stand while they dry.

Panorama

The construction of a 3-D panorama creates a setting where grandchildren can introduce their own characters and scenery.

Age level: 5–12 years

Number of children: any

What you need:

- An old shoebox or other strong box.
- Paint, coloured pencils or felt-tip pens.
- Coloured paper.
- Scissors.
- Glue.
- Plasticine or Blu Tack.
- Small toys and objects.

What to do:

- Your grandchildren can think about the 3-D scene they want to make. What materials will they use to make the figures, creatures and scenery? How can they make a story come alive?
- Turn the box on its side or end so it is accessible to grandchildren and can be viewed by the potential audience.
- Paint the inside of the box. For example, blue for a sea, sky or underwater background, green for a rainforest panorama.
- Draw figures, trees or animals on paper. Leave a tab at the bottom.
- Cut out the figures, trees or animals, leaving the tab on the bottom.
- Bend the tabs back. Put glue on the tabs and glue them into the panorama.

❡ Grandparent tips

- Cellophane or small mirrors make excellent rivers or ponds.
- Craft popsicle sticks can become people.
- Use plasticine or Blu Tack to fasten small toys in position, for example, dinosaurs or rainforest animals.

Stone animal

You will need to collect smooth, light-coloured stones, rocks or pebbles for this activity. Grandchildren can choose a stone with a shape that suggests an animal.

Age level: 3–12 years

Number of children: any

What to collect:
- Stones, creek or riverbed rocks or pebbles.
- Acrylic paints.
- Paintbrushes.
- Clear varnish.

Protective covering for grandchildren and surfaces.

What to do:
- Each grandchild needs to have a good look at the stone they have chosen. What type of animal does it suggest? Is it a mouse, a sleeping bear, a sea monster, a dinosaur, a perching bird, a cow or a sleeping cat or dog? Grandparents can have input here to fire their grandchild's imagination.
- Put a first coat of paint on the animal. A second coat may be needed to ensure a good covering.
- Add details when the first coat of paint is dry. For example, paint fur, legs, feet, scales, a curled-up tail or spines on the stone.
- Allow the paint to dry and add a coat of clear varnish.

Grandparent tip
- Grandchildren can give their finished stone animals as gifts, or use them as paperweights. Stone animals make perfect pets.

Unicorn

A unicorn is a new type of 'hobbyhorse' that many grandparents rode as children. Younger grandchildren can help their grandparents make the unicorn. Older grandchildren can make their own.

Age level: 3–8 years

Number of children: any

What you need:
- A large white plastic bag.
- Felt-tip pens.
- Scraps of coloured paper or felt.
- Scissors.
- Fabric glue.
- Cellophane or fabric fringing.
- A broom or mop handle – cut to a size grandchildren can straddle comfortably.
- Newspaper for stuffing.
- A circle of cardboard.
- Glitter.
- Paint.
- A length of cord or masking tape.
- Ribbons.

What to do:
- Draw a face on the plastic bag.
- Cut out ears from the coloured paper or felt and glue them onto the plastic bag.
- Glue on material scraps to make eyes, nostrils and mouth.
- Cut the cellophane into strips or use fabric fringing and glue them onto the unicorn's head to make a mane.
- Place the head over the broom or mop handle.

⊚ Stuff it with newspaper to make a head shape.

⊚ Make a horn out of the circle of cardboard and stick it onto the unicorn's head.

⊚ Decorate the horn and face with glitter and paint.

⊚ Fasten the unicorn's head firmly onto the broom or mop handle with cord or masking tape.

⊚ Make some reins with ribbons.

💡 Grandparent tips

- Make sure your grandchildren ride their unicorn in a safe area. Watch your ornaments, TV and furniture if the unicorn is galloped indoors.
- Young grandchildren can keep their unicorn stabled at your home.

Bookmark

Grandchildren can use the bookmark they make to mark the pages when they read and share tree books with you.

Age level: 3–12 years

Number of children: any

What you need:

- A piece of cardboard.
- Scissors.
- A ruler.
- Felt-tip pens, coloured pencils or paint.
- Scraps of coloured paper, stickers and glitter.

What to do:

- Measure and cut out a piece of cardboard measuring 20 cm x 8 cm.
- Draw a design on the bookmark.
- Decorate the bookmark with scraps of coloured paper, stickers and glitter.

Grandparent tips

- Bookmarks can be any shape or size. Try making one in felt and decorate it with embroidered stitches or glue on different pieces of coloured felt.
- You can make a mouse by cutting out a flat body shape. Glue on ears and whiskers and add a dangly woollen tail to mark the place in a book.

Body-shape poster

Grandchildren will be able to see their actual size and shape when they make their body-shape poster.

Age level: 3–12 years

Number of children: any

What you need:

- A sheet of paper as big as your grandchild.
- A thick pencil or crayon.
- Paint and brushes.
- Tape to join the sheets of paper.

What to do:

- Place the paper on a smooth hard floor surface. Join several sheets of paper together if necessary.
- Ask your grandchild to lie on the paper. Make sure their fingers are spread out so the pencil can go around each finger.
- Draw around your grandchild with a thick pencil or crayon.
- Now your grandchild can draw or paint their hair, face and clothes on their body shape.
- Cut out the finished shape to pin on the wall.

Grandparent tips

- Grandchildren can take their body-shape poster home or you can keep it. Bring it out from time to time to see how much your grandchild has grown.
- Just for fun, swap roles. You can lie on the floor and your grandchildren can draw around you.

Papier-mâché

Papier-mâché is the art of creating objects by applying layers of paper and glue. This is a sticky but fun way for grandchildren to be creative when they spend time indoors.

Papier-mâché is an activity that works well in four parts. Grandchildren can work on a different step in the process on different visits, or complete an object over a few days when staying over.

Papier-mâché bowls

A papier-mâché bowl is made by applying layers of paper and glue over an existing bowl used as a cast. Grandchildren need to wait until each layer is dry before they continue making their bowl. This is an excellent activity to do when your grandchildren are staying for a few days, or it can be spread over several visits.

Age level: 8–12 years

Number of children: any

What you need:

- Old newspapers.
- Glue (white or PVA glue, flour and water glue, or wallpaper paste all work well).
- A small bowl to mix the paste in or hold the glue.
- Vaseline (petroleum jelly).
- A medium-sized plastic bowl.
- A small paintbrush (2–5 cm).
- Scissors.
- Paints.
- Clear varnish.

What to do:

Step 1

◎ Tear pieces of newspaper into strips.

◎ Mix up some wallpaper paste in the small bowl or pour in some glue.

◎ Spread Vaseline over the outside of the medium-sized plastic bowl so the papier-mâché will peel off easily when completed.

◎ Dip the strips of newspaper into the paste.

◎ Place the strips on the outside of the medium-sized bowl so that they overlap. Be sure to cover every part of the bowl.

◎ Brush the strips with paste and then start another layer of newspaper strips.

Step 2

◎ Allow the first two layers to dry before adding more strips of newspaper.

◎ Add four or five more layers. Allow to dry.

Step 3

◎ When the bowl is dry (the papier-mâché will feel hard to touch), take it off the mould carefully.

◎ Neaten the edges with scissors.

Step 4

◎ When the papier-mâché is completely dry, your grandchildren can paint and decorate their bowl.

◎ Paint the inside, then paint the outside with a contrasting colour.

◎ Use a paintbrush to decorate the bowl with whirls and swirls or any design they might choose.

◎ When the paint is completely dry, apply one or two thin coats of clear varnish to protect the bowl.

💡 Grandparent tip

• Protective covering for grandchildren and surfaces is advised.

Papier-mâché masks

Masks are fun to make. They can be the gateway into a fantastic imaginative world for grandchildren.

Age level: 8–12 years

Number of children: any

What you need:

- ☞ Old newspaper.
- ☞ Wallpaper paste.
- ☞ A small bowl to mix the wallpaper paste in.
- ☞ Vaseline petroleum jelly.
- ☞ A medium-sized bowl, the same width as your grandchild's face.
- ☞ A small paintbrush (2–5 cm).
- ☞ Paint and glitter or other decorations.
- ☞ Pieces of ribbon or thin elastic.

What to do:

- ☼ Follows steps 1, 2 and 3 for making the papier-mâché bowl.
- ☼ When the bowl is dry, cut two slits for the eyes and two small holes to secure the ribbon or elastic.
- ☼ Paint and decorate the mask.
- ☼ Attach pieces of ribbon or thin elastic to hold the mask on your grandchild's head.

💡 Grandparent tips

- Masks can be made to cover your grandchildren's faces for a complete disguise. You could also cut the mask before it is decorated, so it just fits over your grandchildren's eyes.
- Animal masks can be made by adding whiskers, horns, noses and ears.

Puppets

Puppets are magic. They come in all shapes and sizes, and are guaranteed to fascinate grandchildren of all ages.

Very young children will need help when they make their puppets, or you can make them for them. Older grandchildren can create more complex puppets.

Paper finger puppets

Paper finger puppets are quick and easy to make. Grandchildren can create a collection of characters and write a play for their puppets to star in.

Age level: 3–5 years

Number of children: any

What you need:
- ✒ Paper.
- ✒ Pencils or felt-tip pens.
- ✒ Scissors.
- ✒ Sticky tape.

What to do:
- ◎ Draw people on a piece of paper about as long as your grandchild's middle finger.
- ◎ Draw tabs on the people so the paper puppet will wrap around your grandchild's finger.
- ◎ Draw the puppets' faces, clothes, arms and legs.
- ◎ Cut out each puppet.
- ◎ Tape the tabs together. Ensure each puppet is small enough to fit around your grandchild's finger.

> ## 💡 Grandparent tip
> - Cut-off the fingers of old gloves to make longer-lasting finger-puppets. Draw faces on them with felt-tip pens.

Sock puppets

Sock puppets can be stored at your house for a rainy-day performance.

Age level: 5–8 years

Number of children: any

What you need:

- Socks.
- Assorted materials such as felt, ribbon, wool and fabric scraps, buttons, feathers and sequins.
- Fabric glue.
- Needle and cotton.
- Wool.

What to do:

- Give each grandchild a sock to put on their hand.
- Discuss with your grandchildren how they will make their puppet. What will their puppet be – an animal, person or an imagined character? Where will the eyes go? How can they make a mouth? Can your grandchildren move their hand inside the sock to make a mouth?
- The next step is for your grandchildren to select materials, and glue or sew them onto their puppet. A hand inserted into the sock will prevent sewing or gluing both sides of the sock together. Younger children will need your assistance with this.

Grandparent tips

- Use darning needles with big eyes to make threading easy.
- Make multiple characters to use in puppet performances.

Hand puppet characters

Grandchildren can make sets of hand-puppet characters to use in a puppet production. For example, three bears and a girl with golden hair.

Age level: 5–8 years

Number of children: any

What you need:
- White cotton material measuring 20 cm x 15 cm.
- Fabric glue.
- Felt-tip pens.
- Sequins, buttons, wool and felt scraps for decoration.

What to do:
- Fold the piece of material along the long edge and place your grandchild's hand on it.
- Trace around your grandchild's little finger, the three middle fingers together, then the thumb.
- Cut out the puppet leaving room for seams and glue the seams together.
- Turn the material inside out and iron flat.
- Your grandchildren can decorate the puppets using pens and decorative materials such as wool for hair and buttons for eyes.

⬤ Grandparent tip
- Puppets can also be sewn together, if desired.

Puppet theatre

Puppets provide hours of fun when they are used in impromptu or planned performances. You just need a little effort to provide a theatre for your grandchildren's puppet shows.

Age level: 3–5 years

Number of children: any

What you need:

- ✐ An empty cereal or shoebox.
- ✐ Scissors.
- ✐ Coloured paper.
- ✐ Felt-tip pens, paint and brushes.

What to do:

- ◈ Stand the empty cereal or shoebox on its end.
- ◈ Cut out a window near the top of the box for puppets to perform in.
- ◈ Decorate the outside of the theatre with coloured paper, pens or paint.

♀ Grandparent tip

- Make sure the theatre is placed in a position where grandchildren can operate their puppets comfortably.

Simple hand-puppet theatre

Age level: 5–12 years

Number of children: any

What you need:
- Material to fit across a doorway (measure the width of the doorway and double it).
- For length, measure from above your grandchildren's heads when they are kneeling, so they will be hidden when they perform.
- Wire to fit across the doorway.
- 2 curtain hooks.

When this simple prop is not in use, store it in the cupboard for future productions.

What to do:
- Hem the top of the material and thread the wire through.
- Fasten the wire to curtain hooks on each side of the doorway.
- Check the curtain is the correct height (hem the bottom if necessary).

Modelling

Play dough is an excellent modelling material for young grandchildren to use. Start with play dough and commercial modelling products – then move onto the exciting media of clay.

Uncooked play dough

Grandchildren can help with the kneading when you make play dough.

Age level: 3–5 years

Number of children: any

What you need:
- 1½ cups of flour.
- 1 cup of salt.
- 125 ml water.
- Several different food colourings.

What to do:
- Combine the flour, salt and water to make a smooth dough.
- Knead the dough on a floured board to a smooth consistency.
- Divide into sections. Add a different food dye to each section.
- Store different colours of play dough in different containers. Keep in the refrigerator for about a week.

ᴆ Grandparent tip
- Biscuit cutters, plastic knives and popsicle sticks make excellent modelling tools.

Salt dough models

Salt dough is a versatile material for grandchildren to model with. The dough can be baked hard, then painted and varnished. Younger grandchildren will love exploring and experimenting with the dough to see what they can make. Older kids can proceed to activities such as pinching out a pot and making coil pots.

Age level: 5–8 years

Number of children: any

What you need:
- 2 cups of salt.
- 2 cups of plain white flour.
- 1 tablespoon of cooking oil.
- 200 ml water.
- Greased baking tray.
- Paints.
- Clear varnish.

What to do:
- Preheat the oven to 180°C.
- Combine the salt, flour and cooking oil in a bowl.
- Add the water, a little at a time, and mix to a soft dough.
- Sprinkle some flour on the table and place the dough on top. Your grandchildren can now knead the dough until it is smooth and stretchy.
- The next step is for them to model the dough into different shapes. They can make jewellery such as beads or badges, 3-D models of animals or objects, or pots by coiling sausages of dough around a circular flat base.
- Place the shapes on a greased baking tray and bake for about 20 minutes.
- When the shapes cool, they can be painted.
- When the paint has dried, they can be coated with clear varnish.

Caution: Supervise older grandchildren when they use the oven.

⚥ Grandparent tips

- Protect grandchildren and surfaces before they start working with clay.
- Cover tables, and have a sheet of plastic or a tray for each grandchild to work on.
- Prepare a shelf or area where finished work can be stored to dry.
- Keep a sealed container to store clay if 'potting' is going to be an ongoing activity.

Clay pendant

Age level: 5–12 years

Number of children: any

What you need:

- A protected surface to work on.
- Air-dried clay such as Das, or Fimo (available at arts and craft supply shops).
- A skewer.
- Length of cord.
- Paint, glue, decorations and clear varnish.

Children can wear their pendant when they have finished making it or give it to someone special as a gift.

What to do:

- Roll the clay into a smooth ball then press flat.
- Cut it into a small shape for a pendant.
- Make a hole with a skewer to thread the cord through. Remind grandchildren to mark their name or initials on the back of the objects they make.
- Allow the pendant to dry.
- Grandchildren can paint, decorate and varnish the pendant if they wish.

Clay coil pot

Making a coil pot is a great way to introduce your grandchildren to the craft of pottery. You can buy air-dried clay from arts and craft shops or potters' suppliers – they will be able to advise you on how to store it.

Age level: 5–12 years

Number of children: any

What you need:

- A flat board or surface to work on.
- A lump of clay about the size of a grapefruit for each grandchild.
- Water in a small bowl.
- Tools to make designs such as plastic cutlery, bolts and screws, shells and other natural materials, rolling pins, biscuit cutters, popsicle sticks, bottle tops, buttons, cord and string, combs, toothbrushes, net and lace.

What to do:

- Your grandchildren will need to roll the clay with the flat of their hand to make a snake or coils. They can also experiment and make a flat spiral.
- By rolling the coils and spiralling them vertically, your grandchildren will be able to make a coiled pot.
- They can smooth the edges of their pots by using a little water and their fingers.
- The next step is to decorate their pot with their choice of design tools.

Clay pinch pot

Age level: 5–12 years

Number of children: any

What you need:

- A flat board or surface to work on.
- A lump of air-dried clay about the size of a grapefruit for each grandchild.
- Water in a small bowl.
- Tools to make designs.

What to do:

- Roll the clay into a ball.
- Make a hole in the centre.
- Your grandchildren can use their fingers to gradually pinch the clay until it makes a shallow pot shape.
- Using the design tools, they can decorate the outside of the pot with a pattern.
- Place the pot in a warm place to dry.

Jewellery

Your grandchildren will love wearing the jewellery they make. It also makes attractive gifts for them to give to their family.

Materials as simple as cut-up drinking straws and wool make attractive necklaces for very young grandchildren. Older grandchildren can create fabulous jewellery using a variety of materials.

Pasta necklaces and bracelets

Pasta – with holes to thread – makes excellent necklaces and bracelets.

Age level: 5–8 years

Number of children: any

What you need:

☑ String or nylon thread – fishing line is great.
☑ A variety of pasta – macaroni, rigatoni, penne – or just 1 kind of pasta. The pasta must have holes in it.
☑ Paint or felt-tip pens.
☑ Gold or silver paint.

What to do:

⚅ Cut string or strong thread to loosely fit your grandchild's neck or wrists.
⚅ Thread the pasta.
⚅ The pasta jewellery can be painted or decorated using felt-tip pens.
⚅ Exclusive jewellery can be made by spraying the pasta with gold or silver paint.

> 💡 **Grandparent tip**
> - Your grandchildren could also dip pasta into different food colours, and thread it when it is dry. Experiment with a few drops of food colouring in a bowl of water.

Jewelled brooches

Grandchildren can make jewelled brooches for themselves or as gifts for their family and friends.

Age level: 8–12 years

Number of children: any

What you need:
- Scrap of paper and a pencil.
- A sheet of thick card.
- Scissors.
- PVA glue.
- A selection of buttons, shells, beads, sequins, pasta and dried peas.
- A small safety pin.
- Strong tape.

What to do:
- Plan the design of the brooch. It can be a star, square, oval, diamond or the shape of an initial.
- Sketch the design, and the exact size and shape, on scrap paper.
- When your grandchildren are happy with their design, they can draw the outline onto the thick card and cut it out.
- Cover the surface with glue.
- Arrange the sequins, macaroni etc within the shape.
- Leave it to dry.
- Turn the brooch over and attach the safety pin with strong tape or glue.

Oven-baked beads

Oven-baked beads can be used to make colourful and original necklaces. The beads can be made in an afternoon and decorated another time.

Age level: 8–12 years

Number of children: 1

What you need:
- 2 cups of plain flour.
- ½ cup of salt.
- ¾ cup of cold water.
- Nail or thin skewer.
- Acrylic paints.
- Brushes.
- Fishing line.

What to do:
- Preheat oven to 150°C.
- Mix the flour and salt together. Add water.
- Knead the dough for at least 10 minutes on a floured board. The dough needs to be pliable and not fall to bits.
- Your grandchildren can then make interesting bead shapes with the dough.
- Use a nail or skewer to poke a hole in the centre of each bead. Make sure the hole goes right through.
- Bake the beads for 2 or 3 hours until they are hard and dry.
- Paint and decorate the beads.
- When the beads are completely dry, thread them with fishing line to make necklaces or bracelets.

Stick weaving

Stick weaving is a simple form of folk art. It is often called making a God's Eye.

Age level: 8–12 years

Number of children: any

What you need:
- 2 sticks (about 15–20 cm long).
- 3 or 4 different coloured wools.
- Scissors.

What to do:
- Tie the sticks together tightly with a piece of wool to form a cross.
- Join the wool to one stick by looping and knotting it.
- Show your grandchildren how to hold the sticks in one hand, and the weaving wool in the other.
- Moving clockwise, show your grandchildren how to wrap the wool over and around the first stick, then move clockwise to the next stick. Continue to turn the stick, weaving as you work.

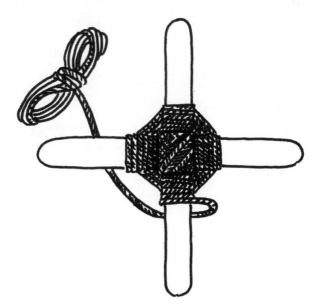

- ◉ Continue wrapping the wool around, creating a diamond-shaped pattern.
- ◉ Knot on new colours of wool, tying one colour to the next to make the stick weaving as attractive as possible.
- ◉ Finish off the stick weaving by tying the wool to the stick.
- ◉ Bells and tassels can be added to the corners to make the stick weaving more decorative.

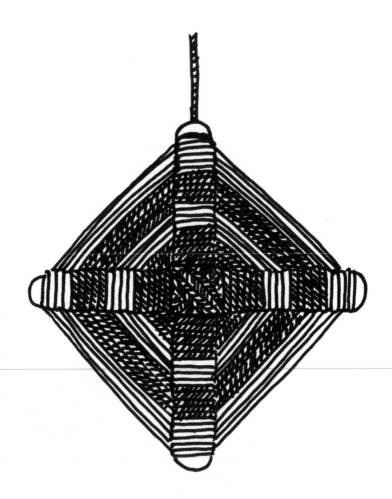

Sewing

As many grandparents know well, the absorbing craft of sewing can give grandchildren many hours of pleasure. It is good to have a few rules, such as :

- Clean hands before beginning to sew.
- Keep needles in a needle-book when they are not in use.
- Keep pins in a pincushion.
- Close scissors when you put them down.
- Carry scissors points down.

Choose sewing projects that can be finished in a short time when your grandchildren start to sew. If the activity becomes tedious, put it away and come back to it another time. Remember: sewing should give grandchildren pleasure. When mistakes happen, help your grandchildren unpick the mistake, and try again. Remember, pinning and tacking helps ensure the success of most sewing projects.

Sewing buttons

Sewing a button onto a garment is a useful skill for grandchildren to learn.

Age level: 8–12 years

Number of children: any

What you need:
- Shirt or similar that is missing a button.
- Pins or a sewing pen.
- A needle.
- Buttons.
- Thread.

What to do:
- Mark the place where the button should go with a pin or sewing pen.
- Thread the needle with thread. Loop the thread and knot the ends.
- Sew the button onto and through the fabric 4 to 6 times.
- Leave the thread slack enough so the button is not squashed tight into the fabric.
- Finish by winding the thread around the back of the button before fastening it off on the reverse side of the fabric.

💡 Grandparent tip
- Buttons make excellent eyes for puppets and toys.

Sewing box

Grandchildren can make an attractive sewing box to keep their sewing materials and tools together. Store it at your house to hold your grandchildren's sewing projects.

Age level: 8–12 years

Number of children: any

What you need:
- An old shoebox with a lid.
- Enough fabric to cover the inside and outside of the box, as well as the lid.
- Fabric glue.
- Braids, ribbons, laces, sequins and beads.

What to do:
- Cut panels of fabric to fit the inside and outside of the box, and the lid.
- Glue the panels carefully in place.
- Decorate the panels with braids, ribbons and laces, sequins and beads.

Suggested equipment for the sewing box
- A small pair of scissors with sharp points for small jobs like snipping threads.
- A medium-sized pair of scissors for cutting out material.
- Threads and cottons in different colours and thicknesses, for example, stranded and soft embroidery cottons.
- Different kinds of needles for sewing through various thicknesses of material and a container to hold them.
- Pins and a pincushion.
- A small magnet to pick up pins.
- A close-fitting thimble for the middle (sewing) finger.
- A soft pencil, tailor's chalk or tailor's chalk pencil for drawing designs on material.
- Ruler and tape measure.

Embroidery

Learning the creative craft of embroidery will give your grandchildren many hours of enjoyment. They will quickly see how they can make marks on fabric with stitches just as they can with a pencil on paper.

Age level: 8–12 years

Number of children: any

What you need:

- Light-coloured material.
- Embroidery ring.
- Sewing pencils.
- Threads and cottons of different sizes and thicknesses.
- Needles – assorted sizes to match threads and cottons.
- Scissors.

What to do:

- Place the material in the embroidery ring to hold it tight.
- Decide on a design and draw it onto the material.
- Thread a needle with a length of thread and knot the end.
- Use a straight stitch to make the design.

Straight stitch

- Put the needle under the ring and push it through the material.
- Make a stitch, as short or as long as you like, by pushing the needle back down through the fabric. You can use this straight stitch to make all sorts of patterns.
- By using different sizes and textures of thread, your grandchildren will be able to create interesting effects.

Running stitch

- Working from right to left, push the needle through the back of the material and into the front.
- Keep the needle level and push it in and out of the material, making sure that the stitches and spaces are equal.
- To finish off, go back to the end of the last stitch and bring the needle through again.
- Cut off the thread at the back, not too close to the material.

Back stitch

- Working from right to left, bring the needle through to the front and then go back, the length of a stitch.
- Push the needle in, pass it under the material, and bring it out, the length of a stitch, in front.
- Draw the needle and thread out.
- Go back to the last stitch and bring the needle forward under the material.

Over sewing

- Working from right to left, bring the needle through from the back of the material to just under the edge of the fabric. Pull the thread through. Repeat.
- This is a good stitch to use to stop a raw edge from fraying, to close a gap, or to join two pieces of felt together.

Satin stitch

- Satin stitch is used to fill in small areas. The stitches go over and over, but are very close together. They may be slanted if you like.
- When pulling the thread through, don't pull it too tight or the material will pucker. Try to keep stitches even.

Echidna pincushion

A friendly echidna pincushion will keep pins safe and ready for use.

Age level: 8–12 years

Number of children: any

What you need:

- A felt-tip pen.
- Tracing paper.
- Scissors.
- Pins.
- 2 pieces of different coloured felt, each measuring 12 cm x 8 cm.
- Black and coloured embroidery cottons.
- A needle with an eye big enough to hold the thread.
- Cotton wool for stuffing.

What to do:

- Trace the outline of an echidna on the paper and cut out a paper pattern (you will be able to find line drawings online).
- Pin the pattern to the felt and cut out the shape. Repeat with a second shape.
- Place both shapes together.
- Over sew the edges, leaving an opening for the cotton wool stuffing.
- Push the stuffing through the opening to make the echidna as fat as possible.
- Press the edges of the opening together and over sew neatly.
- Embroider the nose and eyes of the echidna in satin stitch, using black embroidery cotton.
- Stick the pins in the echidna to make prickles – not too far.

Wool doll

Many grandparents will remember making this simple doll from wool. Your grandchildren can make clothes for the doll from fabric scraps, and furniture from recycled lids, boxes and containers.

Age level: 8–12 years

Number of children: any

What you need:
- Wool (any colour).
- A rectangular piece of cardboard – the length of the cardboard will be the length of the doll.
- Scissors.
- Felt-tip pens.
- Embroidery cottons.
- A needle.

What to do:
- Wind the wool around the card about 30 times.
- Cut all the strands at the bottom end of the cardboard. Remove from the cardboard.
- Plump the top strands into a ball – this is the head. Tie a separate piece of wool where the neck should be.

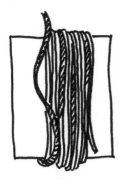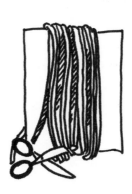

- Separate a few strands of wool on each side and cut them to make them the appropriate length for arms. Tie pieces of wool where the wrists should be.
- To make the body, bulge out the remaining strands. Tie a piece of wool at the bottom of the body.
- Halve the rest of the wool to make the legs.
- To make the feet, tie two more pieces of wool around the ankles.
- Embroider or draw a face on the doll with felt-tip pens.

Knitting

Knitting is a craft that grandchildren will enjoy mastering. Creating a Doctor Who scarf – a very long scarf in many colours – is a good way to start. Choose a variety of brightly coloured, medium ply balls of wool. Plain or garter stitch is an excellent beginner's stitch.

Age level: 8–12 years

Number of children: any

What you need:
- Several balls of multi-coloured wool.
- A pair of knitting needles that will match the ply of the wool selected.
- A large-eyed wool needle.

Casting on
- To cast on, make a loop close to the end of the wool and put it on the left needle. Pull the loop tightly so it just fits.
- Pass the point of the right needle from left to right through the loop on the left needle.
- Pass the wool round the point of the right needle.
- Draw both needle and wool through the loop, to make a loop on the right needle.
- Slip the loop onto the left needle. Take the right needle away.
- Repeat for the number of stitches required. You'll need 20 to 60 stitches, depending on the ply of the wool and thickness of the knitting needles.

Garter stitch or plain knitting
- Hold the needle with the cast-on stitches in your left hand.
- Pass the point of the right needle from left to right through the first loop.
- Pass the wool round the point of the right needle and draw both needle and wool through the loop, making the first loop on the right needle.

- Allow the loop that has been made to drop from the left needle to form the knitting.
- The wool is always held at the back of the work in plain knitting.
- Keep knitting stitch after stitch, row after row, until the scarf reaches the desired length.

Casting off

- Knit two stitches. Pass the first stitch over the second and off the point of the right needle.
- Knit another stitch and pass the stitch already on the needle over this and off the point.
- This is repeated until all except the last stitch are cast off.
- The wool is cut and the end is drawn through the remaining stitch.
- The end of the wool is darned with a wool needle into the fabric.

Grandparent tips

- Very young knitters can knit a scarf for a doll or teddy with very few stitches and a thicker ply wool.
- Colour or mark needles (using a dab of paint or nail polish) so young grandchildren can tell their left needle from their right.
- Pick up stitches as soon as your grandchildren drop them.
- Continually count stitches. Children's knitting tends to get wider and wider instead of longer and longer.

Musical instruments

Age level: 3–7 years

Number of children: any

What you need:

✐ Anything that will make a sound (see below).

Grandchildren can use their homemade instruments for individual performances or to set up their own pop group, band or orchestra. Grandparents can help younger children make their instruments. Ideas for musical instruments include:

- The kitchen cupboard is an excellent source of musical instruments for grandchildren who want to play in a band.
- Two saucepan lids banged together make a great set of cymbals.
- A frying pan tapped with a fork can contribute a good rhythm.
- A cheese grater tied to a piece of string and played with a teaspoon makes an interesting sound.
- Various types of empty bottles will add extra notes when blown across the top.

Bottle-top bells

Bottle-top bells are fun to make, and they make great music!

Age level: 5–12 years

Number of children: any

What you need:

- ☝ 5 metal bottle tops.
- ☝ A length of wood measuring 30 cm x 2 cm.
- ☝ A hammer.
- ☝ 5 small nails.

What to do:

- ■ Hammer the bottle tops to the flat side of the wood with small nails. The bottle tops should be just touching. Don't hammer too tightly or they won't rattle.

Bottle chimes

You can make music on these bottle chimes by listening to the high or low notes as you tap the bottles filled with water.

Age level: 3–8 years

Number of children: any

What you need:

- 8 glass bottles – the same size and shape. Juice bottles are ideal.
- A ruler.
- A felt-tip pen.
- A jug of water.
- A wooden spoon.

What to do:

- Place the bottles in a straight line on a table. Make sure they are close together but not touching.
- With a ruler, measure up from the bottom of each bottle, drawing a line with the felt-tip pen.
- Measure 20 mm up on the first bottle, 40 mm up on the second bottle, then continue by increasing the measure by 20 mm each time on the remaining bottles.
- Using the jug of water, fill each bottle to the marked line.
- Take the wooden spoon and tap each bottle gently.
- Listen to the notes getting higher or lower, depending on the amount of water in the bottle.

Grandparent tips

- Grandchildren can use felt-tip pens and paints to decorate their instruments.
- Make sure the decorations are dry before players start using their instruments.

Musical rattle

A musical instrument can be ready to rattle and make music in a very short time.

Age level: 3–6 years

Number of children: any

What you need:

- A plastic drink bottle or a container with a lid.
- Rice, macaroni or small pebbles.

What to do:

- Wash the bottle or container and lid well.
- Make sure it is dry inside and out.
- Put in a handful of rice, macaroni or small pebbles.
- Screw or fasten the lid on tightly and shake!

Drum

Age level: 3–7 years

Number of children: any

What you need:

- Scissors.
- A clean ice cream container with a lid.
- Cord or string for the neck strap.
- Coloured paper.
- 2 sticks of dowel 30 cm long.
- 2 thumb tacks.

What to do:

- To make the drum, use scissors to make two holes in the opposite sides of the ice cream container, just below where the lid fits.
- Measure the length of cord to fit through one hole, around the drummer's neck and down through the other hole with a little extra for tying.
- Thread the cord and tie off both ends.
- Fit the lid firmly in place.
- To make the drumsticks, cut the coloured paper into equal lengths, about 50 cm long by 1 cm wide.
- Attach 4 lengths of coloured paper to the end of each dowel stick with a thumbtack.
- Now your grandchildren are ready to walk to the beat of their own drum!

Outdoor games and activities

Introduction

Spending time outdoors with your grandchildren is fun. Set aside a safe area in your garden or backyard where your grandchildren can play safely, using their imagination and expending lots of energy. If your own outdoor area is limited, visit your nearest local park to see if it is suitable, and go there often when your grandchildren are with you.

Grandparents and grandchildren alike can have fun **outdoors** in most kinds of weather if wearing suitable protective clothing. However, many outdoor activities can also be modified to suit a venue such as a garage or veranda. Substituting equipment can quickly change an outdoor activity into an indoor one – for example, use a scrunched-up paper ball and a wastepaper basket to play indoor basketball.

Find a spot in your home where you can store inexpensive equipment for outdoor games and activities. **Outdoor equipment** could include the following:

- Balls of all shapes and sizes (for example, tennis balls, tactile balls, rubber balls, basketballs, soccer balls and footballs).
- Bats of all shapes and sizes (for example, paddle bats, softball bats and rounders bats).
- Sets for cricket, badminton or shuttlecock, table tennis and golf.

- Portable sports nets.
- Tennis racquets and plastic hockey sticks.
- Tether tennis or totem tennis.
- Chalk for making court markings (it washes off in the rain).
- Ropes, for skipping and jumping.
- Quoits.
- Frisbees.
- Boxes, old sheets and curtains etc. to make cubby houses, castles, spaceships and pirate ships.
- Gardening tools.

⚇ Grandparent tip

- Children's sports equipment makes great gifts for grandchildren.

Blowing bubbles

Blowing bubbles is a magical activity for children young and old, especially on a lovely sunny day.

Age level: 3–8 years

Number of children: any

What you need:

- 2 tablespoons of dishwashing liquid.
- 1 cup of hot water.
- 1 tablespoon of glycerine (available at chemists).
- An airtight plastic bottle or container with a lid.
- A pipe cleaner.

What to do:

- Pour the dishwashing liquid, water and glycerine into the bottle.
- Put the lid on tightly and shake well.
- Twist an end of the pipe cleaner into a loop to form a wand.
- Dip the wand into the bubble mixture then blow.

Grandparent tips

- You can keep the bubble mixture in a bottle or container until needed.
- To make **giant bubbles**, triple the recipe ingredients and mix together in a big bowl. Add a few extra squirts of dishwashing liquid. To make a giant wand, twist a wire coat hanger into a loop.
- To make **coloured bubbles**, add 2 or 3 drops of food colouring to the bowl of water. If you have several bowls of water and various bottles of food colouring you can make multi-coloured bubbles.

Painting with water

Painting with water is a brilliant yet simple outdoor activity for young grandchildren on a hot day.

Age level: 3–5 years

Number of children: 1 or more

What you need:
- A small paint bucket.
- Water.
- A paintbrush or pastry brush.

What to do:
- Half-fill the bucket with water and encourage your grandchildren to 'paint' the exterior walls of your house, the paths, trees, fences etc.

Flying kites

Flying a kite is an exciting experience for you and your grandchildren. Buy a kite or, even better, build one together. Keep it handy and make the most of kite weather – a breezy day is perfect for kite-flying.

Kites come in all sorts of **fantastic shapes and sizes**. As well as diamond-shaped kites, there are three-dimensional, box-shaped designs and even kites that are shaped like birds, dragons or people. Encourage your grandchildren to experiment with different designs.

Kites fly well in light or moderate wind – very windy days are generally not the best days to fly a kite. When you let your kite out in a moderate wind, it will rise up. Jerk the string and the kite will swoop. If the wind drops, so will the kite. Your grandchildren can make their kite rise by pulling in some of the string or by running to pull the kite through the air. If your model fails, try a different kite design on another day.

To **fly your kite safely**, consider the following:

- Always choose an open area to fly a kite. Avoid roads and other busy places.
- Don't fly kites over houses. Kites crashing into houses or gardens are unpopular intruders.
- Watch out for trees.
- Make sure there are no electric poles, towers or overhead wires nearby. Let go of your kite immediately if the kite or its string gets tangled in a power line.
- Don't fly kites in wet, rainy weather or when thunderstorms are about.
- Protect your grandchildren's hands whey they are flying a kite. Make sure the string is wound around a cardboard tube or small plastic bottle. They should wear gloves when flying big, strong kites.

Many people fly kites in **competitions** – as individuals, in pairs or in teams. Find out where these exciting contests are held by checking in your local newspaper or with your local council and take your grandchildren along to watch. It's a wonderful sight to see the kite-flyers controlling their kites, making them dip, dive and soar as they participate in these dazzling events in the sky. Perhaps one day you and your grandchildren will be able to compete!

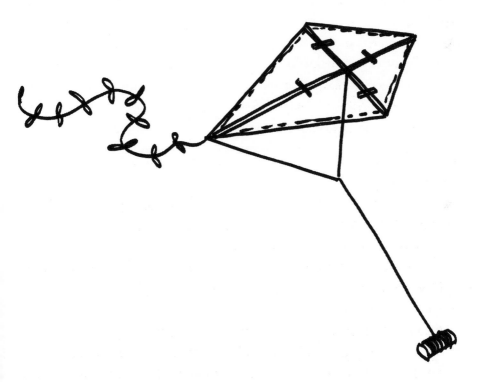

Diamond-shaped kite

The diamond-shaped kites that you made when you were young are still a successful model for your grandchildren to make and fly.

Age level: 5–12 years

Number of children: any

What you need:

- Two pieces of timber dowel of equal length – one for the spine, one for the bow or cross stick.
- String or strong glue for binding.
- Light material such as strong paper or plastic for covering the kite.
- Staples or strong sticky tape.
- String, pieces of plastic or paper, old stockings or strips of cloth to make a tail.
- Control string (also called a bridle) to change the angle of the kite.
- A reel of strong string or nylon fishing line to hold the kite in the air.

What to do:

- Bind the spine and cross stick together with string two or three times or glue the spine and cross stick together.
- Cut a cover for the kite frame from strong paper or plastic. Allow a margin of 4 cm in every direction for turnovers.
- Fasten the cover to the frame with staples or strong sticky tape.
- Cut a piece of string to make a tail. It needs to be six times the width of the kite (in length).
- Tie the pieces of plastic, paper or cloth to the tail.
- Fix the tail to your kite with staples or sticky tape.
- Fasten your control string (bridle) to the kite and a reel of strong string or nylon fishing line to hold the kite in the air.

Plastic bag kite

Age level: 8–12 years

Number of children: 1 or more

What you need:

- A small rubbish-bin liner.
- Scissors.
- 2 lengths of dowel measuring 60 cm long, or sticks.
- Strong sticky tape.
- A ball of string.
- Cardboard tube or stick.
- A pen.
- A ruler.

Older grandchildren can use their measuring skills to make this kite themselves.

What to do:

- Cut the plastic bag open. Measure and cut the shape that's shown in the diagram.
- Tape the 2 lengths of dowel or sticks to the plastic bag as shown in the diagram.

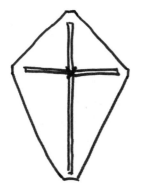 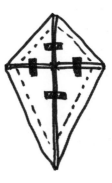

- Strengthen the corners by folding the bag and taping with sticky tape.
- Attach a 90 cm piece of string to each corner.
- Wind a long length of string onto the cardboard tube and tie it to the kite's strings.
- Now the kite is ready to fly.

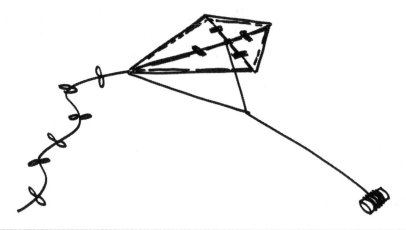

♀ Grandparent tip

- Choose a large open area to test-fly the kite. Hold the kite by its bridle so the wind catches it. Release the line evenly so the kite flies steadily.

Paper airplanes

Aeronautical grandparents will have happy memories of making and flying paper airplanes when they were young. It's an activity that will intrigue grandchildren of all ages.

Flying paper airplanes is educational as well as fun, as it demonstrates the simple principles of flight. Together, you can use books or the internet to research the science of flight. Your **flight instructions** are as follows.

- Encourage grandchildren to experiment with different take-off techniques.
- Where is the best place to hold the plane to get the best flight?
- Can they find the point of balance?
- Can they throw their plane forward smoothly?

☺ Grandparent tips

- Fold the paper airplane on a flat, hard surface.
- Sharp creases help a plane to fly well, so always press creases firmly. Use the back of your nail or a ruler to strengthen the creases.
- Younger grandchildren will need your help when making their models.
- You can demonstrate how to make models for older grandchildren, and then let them develop their own original designs.

Basic paper airplane

All you really need to make an amazing paper airplane is paper. If your plane doesn't fly well, make another airplane with fresh paper and try again.

Age level: 5–12 years

Number of children: any

What you need:

- A piece of strong paper measuring 30 cm long x 20 cm wide.
- Sticky tape.
- Scissors.

What to do:

- Fold the piece of paper in half lengthwise (see Figure 1).
- Open the paper flat and turn down the two top corners to meet the centre fold (see Figure 2).
- Fold the two sides in once again towards the centre (see Figure 3).
- Close up (see Figure 4).
- Fold the two wings outwards (see Figure 5).
- Fold a piece of sticky tape across the nose of the airplane. Cut two flaps in the tail and fold up (see Figure 6).

Caution: Always throw a pointed-nose airplane away from people.

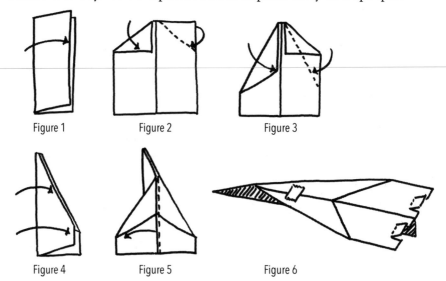

Figure 1   Figure 2   Figure 3

Figure 4   Figure 5   Figure 6

Paper helicopter

A paper helicopter is quick to make and fun to launch from small heights.

Age level: 5–12 years

Number of children: any

What you need:

- A piece of paper measuring 25 cm long x 6 cm wide.
- Scissors.

What to do:

- Make three cuts in the piece of paper: one long horizontal cut and two smaller vertical cuts (see diagram).
- Fold along the dotted lines and bend the end over.
- Fold out the two flaps at the top to make the blades.

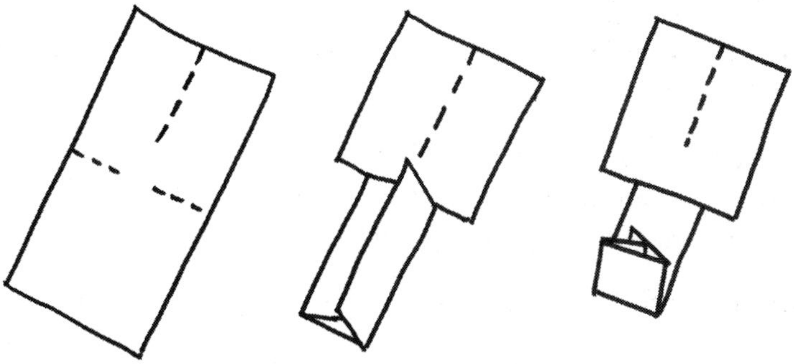

- Launch the helicopter from a height and watch it whirl around as it falls to the ground.

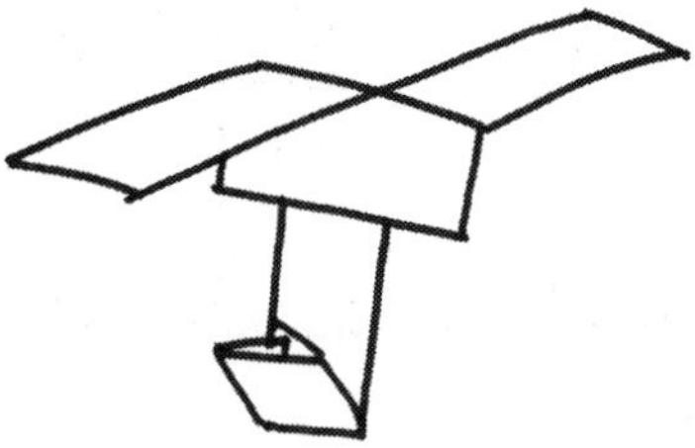

Grandparent tip

- Hold onto your grandchildren if they need to stand on chairs to launch their helicopters.

Paper windmill

Young grandchildren will enjoy making this paper windmill. When it's complete they can tie the windmill to their bike or run with it and watch it spin.

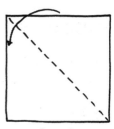

Figure 1

Age level: 3–12 years

Number of children: 1 or more

What you need:

Figure 2

- 📝 A square of paper.
- 📝 Scissors.
- 📝 A pin.
- 📝 A straight stick.

What to do:

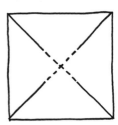

Figure 3

- ✿ Fold the paper in half, corner to corner (see Figure 1).
- ✿ Open the paper and fold it again the other way (see Figure 2).
- ✿ Cut along the fold line from each corner, halfway to the middle of the square (see Figure 3).
- ✿ Fold each corner to overlap in the centre (see Figure 4).
- ✿ Stick a pin through the folded corners and into the stick (see Figure 5), leaving enough room for the windmill to spin easily on the stick.

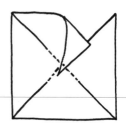

Figure 4

Figure 5

Homemade telephone

Young grandchildren will enjoy having conversations with you outdoors when they use this easy-to-make, homemade telephone.

Age level: 3–8 years

Number of children: any

What you need:

- Two empty yoghurt pots.
- A couple of metres of string.

What to do:

- Punch a hole in the bottom of each pot.
- Thread an end of string through one of the pots and tie a knot in it. Do the same with the other pot.
- Holding the string taut, speak into one pot while your grandchild holds the other pot to their ear.
- The vibrations from your voices will carry your messages along the string.

Outdoor cubby houses

A **cubby house, den or hut** in your garden or backyard will provide many happy hours of playing for your grandchildren. Children of all ages love hidden spots where they can create hideaways or a space of their very own. If you are a builder or handyman extraordinaire, you can design and build a tree house or cubby that can be a permanent fixture in your garden.

Temporary cubby houses are great spaces to play in. They can be quickly erected in the garden whenever your grandchildren visit.

- Peg a tarpaulin or bedspread over the clothesline so it hangs down to the ground on each side. Secure the ends to the ground with small stakes or hold it in place with bricks.
- String a rope between two trees or poles. Drape a rug or tarpaulin over it. Use heavy bricks to secure the rug to the ground.
- Sew strong material around the edges of a beach umbrella. (Make sure the beach umbrella is securely screwed into the ground when you put it up.)
- The large boxes that home appliances are transported in make excellent portable cubbies. Doors and windows can be cut into them, and your grandchildren can then paint and decorate them, inside and out. Erect them on a balcony or in the garden, then fold them away in the garage when not in use.

Alternatively, clear a safe area in your garage or shed where your grandchildren can create their own little world and play in their own space. You may be able to find some old cushions or tables and chairs that they can use.

Teepee

A teepee or wigwam is easy to erect when your grandchildren visit, and just as easy to store when not in use.

Age level: 5–12 years

Number of children: any

What you need:

- Three strong sticks, about as tall as your grandchildren.
- Rope or strong string.
- An old sheet or curtain.
- Paint.
- Brush.

What to do:

- Tie the sticks loosely together near one end with rope or strong string.
- Arrange two sticks to form an X. The third stick will rest in the fork of the X.
- Open out the sticks at the bottom as far as they will go. They will hold the teepee firmly in place.
- Cut a hole in the middle of the sheet or curtain so it will go around the sticks.
- Your grandchildren can paint the outside of the teepee with signs or shapes.

Grandparent tip

- Large safety pins are useful to close the entrance to the teepee.

Gardening

Many grandparents list **gardening as one of their favourite pastimes and pleasures** in life. Encourage your grandchildren to garden with you, and help them to learn how to nurture and grow their own plants.

If you have the kind of garden that is open during Garden Week, it's wise to take a few precautions to **grandchildproof your garden**. Erecting subtle barriers to define plant borders is often all that is needed to protect your precious garden beds. It's also a good idea to talk to your grandchildren about your garden. Explain how precious plants are and that they need loving care – just like grandchildren!

If you don't have a garden, take your grandchildren along to a **local park or your city's botanical gardens** to enjoy the sights, smells and colours of plants and flowers. Don't forget that there are plenty of simple activities connected with growing plants that grandchildren can do without needing to be in an actual garden.

♀ Grandparent tip

- If necessary, replace a dead plant with a live one that's similar to prevent a young gardener's heartache and to sustain their enthusiasm for gardening.

Growing carrot tops

Age level: 5–12 years

Number of children: 1 or more

What you need:
- A carrot with a stump of green stems left on top.
- A saucer.

Gardening with young grandchildren can be as simple as growing carrot tops and vegetables from seeds. Your grandchildren will be able to watch them grow and experience the pleasure of gardening for the first time. When your grandchildren grow carrot tops, they will be able to watch a brand-new leafy carrot top emerge and develop.

What to do:
- Cut the top off the carrot.
- Sit the carrot top in a saucer of water on a sunny windowsill.
- The carrot tops will sprout in about 1–2 weeks. Leaves can be used in salads, soups or as a garnish!

Growing seeds

Choose large seeds such as beans or peas so your grandchildren can learn about what is happening under the ground when seeds start to grow. They can watch as each seed grows whiskery roots and tiny green shoots.

Age level: 5–12 years

Number of children: any

What you need:
- Cotton wool.
- A saucer.
- Seeds.

What to do:
- Place a layer of cotton wool on a saucer and soak it with water.
- Put a few seeds on the damp cotton wool.
- Leave the saucer in a warm, light place.
- Make sure the cotton wool is kept moist.
- The seeds will sprout in about 1–2 weeks, after which time you can plant them outside.

Grow-and-eat eggshell garden

Grandchildren will enjoy growing seeds indoors in these amusing containers – and they'll be able to eat the results of their gardening. Cress grows very fast from seed and tastes good. It grows well in a shallow container: just keep the soil damp and position the container on a sunny windowsill.

Age level: 3–8 years

Number of children: any

What you need:

- ▤ Clean, empty eggshells. You can save these up when you're cooking.
- ▤ Felt-tip pens.
- ▤ Cotton wool.
- ▤ A packet of cress seeds.
- ▤ Eggcups.

What to do:

- ◉ Decorate the eggshells with felt-tip pens.
- ◉ Moisten the cotton wool with water and place it inside the eggshells.
- ◉ Sprinkle some cress seeds on top of the cotton wool.
- ◉ Stand the eggshells in eggcups and leave on a window ledge.
- ◉ Make sure the cotton wool is kept moist.
- ◉ The eggshell gardens will grow in just a few days.
- ◉ When the cress is as long as your finger, snip some off and serve it to your grandchildren in a salad or sandwich.

Submarines

Age level: 3–8 years

Number of children: any

What you need:

- ✐ One long bread roll for each person
- ✐ Butter or margarine
- ✐ Fillings (see below for ideas)

Your grandchildren can harvest their crops of cress to make their own submarines – long bread rolls that are stuffed with your favourite fillings, for example:

- ▪ Mashed tuna mixed with mayonnaise, sweet corn and cress.
- ▪ Mashed hard-boiled egg, either mixed with mayonnaise or plain, topped with cress.
- ▪ Cooked chicken and yoghurt, topped with cress.
- ▪ Sliced salami and tomato, topped with cress.
- ▪ Chopped celery and grated carrot mixed with cottage cheese, natural yoghurt and cress.
- ▪ Lettuce, tomato, cress and other salad ingredients.

What to do:

- ◉ Slice the rolls lengthways, but not quite all the way through.
- ◉ Butter your roll.
- ◉ Pile on the fillings of your choice.
- ◉ Close the top over.
- ◉ Wrap in cling film or foil until ready to be eaten.

💡 Grandparent tip

- Alfalfa seeds can be used instead of cress seeds.

Edible forest

Your grandchildren can grow an edible forest on a plate.

Age level: 3–8 years

Number of children: 1 or more

What you need:

- Cotton wool.
- A large plate.
- Cress or alfalfa seeds.
- Small toy animal.

What to do:

- Arrange the cotton wool in a circle around the edge of the plate. Moisten it well, then sprinkle with cress seeds.
- Put the plate in a warm, light place such as a windowsill.
- When the seeds begin to sprout, place a small toy animal in the centre of the plate.
- Soon you will be able to cut the forest, revealing the toy animal once again, and use your edible forest to make sandwiches.

Plate garden

Age level: 3–8 years

Number of children: 1 or more

What you need:
- Pencil and paper.
- An old large dinner plate, tin lid or seed tray.
- Potting soil.
- Gardening gloves for grandchildren and grandparents.
- Collection of small twigs, leaves and flower heads.
- Scissors.
- Small pebbles.
- A small dish.

Your grandchildren will find this mini landscape design project a fascinating activity to undertake.

What to do:
- Use the pencil and paper to work out a design for your plate garden. Where will you put the flowerbeds, trees, paths and a pond?
- Fill the plate or container with soil (don't forget to use gloves). Dampen it a little.
- Trim the flower heads, small twigs and leaves and place them in position on the plate.
- Use the pebbles to make a path.
- Push the small dish into the soil and fill it with water to make a pond.

Landscape gardening hints
- When flower heads die, they can be replaced with new ones.
- Use different flowers, leaves and twigs to make seasonal gardens throughout the year.
- Add small toys such as ducks, turtles and birds to your garden.

Potting plants

Growing plants in pots is a great activity for gardeners of all ages who are short on garden space. Pot plants thrive on a balcony, or they can be given away as presents.

Age level: 3–12 years

Number of children: any

What you need:

- A selection of seedlings:
  - Petunia or marigold seedlings are fast growing and produce bright flowers.
  - Herbs such as thyme, mint, parsley and sage smell and taste good.
  - Lettuces come in many varieties and are fast-growing vegetables. They can be harvested leaf by leaf and eaten in sandwiches or salads.
- A collection of pots or containers, for example, tin cans or plastic ice-cream containers.
- House paint.
- A hammer and large nail.
- Small stones.
- Good-quality potting mix.
- Gardening gloves for grandchildren and grandparents.
- Gardening tools – an old fork and spoon work well.
- Plant fertiliser.

What to do:

- Buy seedlings from a garden shop. Ask for advice about plants that will grow well where you or your grandchildren live.
- Decorate the pots or containers with paint. (House paint stays on well outdoors.)
- When the pots are dry, hammer holes into the bottom of the pots using a large nail. This will prevent the plants from becoming waterlogged.
- Pour in small stones to stop the holes from getting blocked with soil.

◎ Half-fill the pots with potting mix. (Don't forget to wear gloves!)

◎ Using your gardening tools, plant the seedlings in the pots.

◎ Gently pack the soil around each plant.

◎ Water each plant with a cup of water and sprinkle them with fertiliser.

💡 Grandparent tip

- Your grandchildren can take their potted plants home. Follow the development of their plants by phone, fax, mail or e-mail.

Growing bulbs in pots

Age level: 3–8 years

Number of children: any

What you need:
- Gardening gloves for grandchildren and grandparents.
- Potting soil.
- A deep bowl or pot.
- Bulbs.
- A plastic bag.

Autumn is the time to plant bulbs so they will be ready for spring blooming. Visit a garden shop with your grandchildren and choose bulbs such as daffodils and tulips that will grow well in pots.

What to do:
- Using gloves, place a layer of potting soil in the container.
- Sit the bulbs on the soil so their points come nearly to the top of the bowl.
- Cover the bulbs with more soil.
- Leave the bowl in a cool, dark place for two months.
- Keep the soil damp. A plastic bag placed over the top of the bowl or pot will help.
- Keep watch, and when the first shoots show, move the bowl to a sunny windowsill.
- Wait and watch for the flowers to appear.

Growing a bulb in a jar

Help your grandchildren grow a bulb in a jar of water. They can watch the bud and roots grow as the plant feeds on the food stored in the bulb.

Age level: 3–8 years

Number of children: 1 or more

What you need:

- ☑ An empty yoghurt container.
- ☑ A knife.
- ☑ An empty jar.
- ☑ 1 tulip or daffodil bulb.

What to do:

- ⚙ Cut out the bottom of the yoghurt container with a knife.
- ⚙ Fit the yoghurt container into the top of the jar.
- ⚙ Place the bulb, pointed end up, into the yoghurt container. It needs to be able to sit in the container without falling out.
- ⚙ Fill the jar with enough water to cover the bottom of the bulb.
- ⚙ Keep the jar in a dark place until the roots are 10 cm long.
- ⚙ Remove the jar to a light position and watch your bulb bloom.

💡 **Grandparent tip**

- It's best to help your grandchildren cut out the bottom of the yoghurt container.

Grandchildren's gardens

If your grandchildren visit regularly, give them a patch of your garden to look after. They can sow seeds and seedlings, and watch their plants as they grow.

Age level: 3–12 years

Number of children: any

What you need:

- A hat, gardening gloves and sunscreen.
- Gumboots in winter and protective shoes in summer.
- A child-sized garden fork, trowel and spade. Paint the handles in bright colours to prevent them from being lost. Show your grandchildren how to care for their tools. Store them in a special place for safekeeping until the next visit.
- A small watering can.
- A bucket to carry tools, seedlings, weeds etc.

What to do:

- Choose a sunny spot in your garden. Make sure it has well-dug soil mixed with manure, so plants will grow relatively quickly.
- Visit a plant nursery and let your grandchildren choose the plants they want to grow. Steer them to plants that are easy to look after and will take tough treatment.
- Forget a harmonious, colour coordinated garden. Children will enjoy selecting bright flowers of assorted colours.
- Protective barriers such as chicken wire will help a delicate plant get a good start.
- Combining flowers, vegetables and herbs provides interest through the seasons.
- Use a combination of fast-sprouting seeds, seedlings and plants in flower so your grandchildren can see quick results. Fast-growing plants will help them see the connection between a seed and the young plant that's developing.
- Choose a mix of perennials and annuals. Perennials add year-round interest while annuals provide a seasonal splash of colour.

Growing fruit and vegetables

One of the best ways to encourage your grandchildren to eat fruit and vegetables is if they grow them themselves, and then pick them straight from the garden.

- Radishes give fast results. They germinate in about a week and are ready to harvest in 6–8 weeks.
- Lettuces will also be ready to eat in 6–8 weeks.
- Carrots provide a surprise when taken from the soil. Grandchildren can help to thin out young carrots that are good to eat.
- Sweet corn, beans and peas grow quickly and are easily picked.
- Strawberries and other berries can be grazed as children play in the garden.
- Tiny tomatoes that grow as big as cherries grow well in a sunny spot in a garden bed or large pot. Your grandchildren can pick and eat them when they are ripe.

Garden salad with dressing

A garden salad is especially tempting if your grandchildren have helped to grow the 'green stuff'.

Age level: 3–12 years

Number of children: any

What you need:

- A tablespoon.
- A screw-top jar.
- A knife.
- A chopping board.
- A grater.
- A large bowl.

For the dressing

2 tablespoons olive oil
2 tablespoons vinegar
pinch of mustard
freshly ground black pepper
pinch of sugar

For the salad

½ crisp lettuce
¼ cucumber
2 carrots
2 tomatoes
2 sticks celery
1 tablespoon chopped parsley

What to do:

- **For the dressing**, put everything in a screw-top jar and shake it well.
- **To make the salad**, shred the lettuce, dice the cucumber, grate the carrots and chop the tomatoes and celery. Finely chop the parsley.
- Mix all the vegetables in a large bowl, pour on some salad dressing, add the parsley and toss the salad.

Grandparent tips

- Add any other fresh vegetables, fruits, nuts, seeds or cheese cubes.
- Child-friendly knives can be found in kitchen stores.

Fruit salad

Fruit is a top-of-the-list health food for grandchildren. It comes in its own recyclable package and is perfect for picnics and take-away snacks. Maybe you can use fruit from your own garden!

Age level: 3–12 years

Number of children: any

What you need:
- A knife.
- A chopping board.
- A large bowl.
- A spoon.
- A citrus juicer.

Ingredients:

2 oranges

fresh fruits in season such as grapes, bananas, peaches, pears, apples, melons, pineapple or strawberries

ice cream or yoghurt, to serve

What to do:
- Wash the fruit under the tap if appropriate.
- Carefully cut the fruit into chunks, except the oranges. (Recycle the peels, seeds and cores into your compost bin.)
- Stir the fruit chunks together in a large bowl.
- Cut the oranges in half and squeeze over the fruit salad using a citrus juicer.
- Stir until the fruit is coated with orange juice.
- Chill in the refrigerator until ready to serve.
- Serve in individual dishes, plain or with ice cream or yoghurt.

Fruit kebabs

Age level: 3–12 years

Number of children: any

What you need:
- A vegetable peeler.
- A small sharp knife.
- 4–6 wooden 15 cm skewers.

Ingredients:

3 bananas

2 apples

2 kiwi fruit

1 punnet of strawberries, washed

ice cream or yoghurt, to serve

What to do:

- Wash the fruit under the tap if appropriate.
- Use a vegetable peeler to peel the apples and kiwi fruit.
- Chop the fruit into 3 cm pieces.
- Arrange the fruit on skewers, making sure you have a variety of fruit on each skewer.
- Serve with ice cream or yoghurt.

Energetic games

Your grandchildren will enjoy making their own temporary sports equipment – and it's a great money saver. Children thrive on games they can play outdoors, especially those that involve a variety of movements: hopping, skipping, running, jumping, balancing, throwing and catching. Energetic games help develop children's hand–eye coordination and other physical skills. Another positive benefit is that they consume heaps of excess energy.

Age level: 3–12 years

Number of children: 1 or more

What you need:

- ▧ Make excellent bats or raquets with rolled-up newspaper secured with sticky tape.
- ▧ Crush paper and bind it with masking tape to make a temporary ball that will not escape too far.
- ▧ Use ice cream containers turned upside down to define boundaries or act as targets. If it's windy, use them the right-way up filled with sand or water. Plastic soft drink bottles filled with sand or water also work well.

ꙮ Grandparent tips

- Paint or chalk a set of stumps on the garden fence.
- Draw a line with paint or chalk on the garage wall to resemble a tennis net.
- If your playing area is restricted, use plastic sports equipment. (It's harder to hit a ball over the fence with plastic equipment!)
- Watch your own physical wellbeing. It's quite acceptable to supervise your grandchildren from a nearby seat while you have a cup of tea or coffee!

Beanbags

Age level: 3–12 years

Number of children: any

What you need:
- Cardboard measuring 10 cm square.
- Strong fabric.
- Scissors.
- A needle and thread.
- A small plastic ziplock bag.
- Rice or lentils.

Small beanbags are useful to have stored away in the shed or cupboard. They are safe objects for young grandchildren to throw and catch, and older children can use them to try their skills at juggling. You can make these small beanbags yourself or help older grandchildren to make them.

What to do:
- Using the square piece of cardboard as a template, cut two squares of fabric for each beanbag.
- With the reverse sides of the material facing outwards, hand (or machine) sew the two squares of material together along 3 sides.
- Turn the beanbag inside out so the right sides of the material are now on the outside.
- Fill the plastic bag with rice or lentils.
- Place the filled plastic bag inside the beanbag.
- Pinch the top edge of the beanbag and sew shut firmly.

Grandparent tips
- Three or more beanbags make excellent objects for young jugglers.
- An easy-to-make beanbag can be made by using old socks. Fill a sock with dried beans. Tuck it inside its mate so the beans won't fall out. Stitch or glue the sock to make the beanbag secure.

Obstacle courses

Obstacle courses are great fun for children of all ages. Set up an obstacle course using everyday objects in your garden or backyard. Include obstacles that will provide your grandchildren with different ways of moving: on and off, through, around, between, forwards and backwards, in and out.

Age level: 3–12 years

Number of children: 1 or more

What you need:

- A trampoline or an old cot mattress for bouncing on or across.
- Old tyres placed on a flat surface for stepping or moving through.
- A ladder placed flat on the ground to jump into with feet together or to balance on from rung to rung.
- Boxes for hopping inside and over, and running around.
- Chairs, tables, hoops, stairs, ropes etc.
- Three chairs in a row for walking over or crawling through.
- A table draped with a cloth for climbing through.
- A hoop hanging from a tree with beanbags to throw through.
- String tied above the ground between two chairs or trees for jumping over or climbing under.
- Chalk lines on paved paths to walk or balance on.
- Balls (for example, rolled-up socks) to throw in a washing basket.
- Old pillowslips or sacks to wear and jump in.
- A tarpaulin held in place with tent pegs to wriggle under.
- A board resting on two old tyres for balancing on.

You don't need to change the obstacles to **make the course harder or easier**. You can challenge your grandchildren's physical skills by altering the way they need to move through the obstacles, for example, walking forwards is easy, walking backwards is harder. They can walk, crawl, jump, run and hop through the course. You can add skills to the course such as throwing, catching, tossing or kicking a ball or beanbag while they move through the obstacles.

Grandparent tip

- Set up a table with oranges, a citrus juicer and plastic cups so your grandchildren can make themselves an orange juice at the finishing post.

Stilts

Walking and balancing on stilts is a challenging activity. Younger grandchildren can help you to make these stilts, and you can supervise older grandchildren as they make their own sets.

Age level: 5–12 years

Number of children: any

What you need:
- Two 825 g cans (empty).
- A hammer.
- House paint and a paintbrush.
- A large screwdriver.
- Nylon cord or rope.

What to do:
- Wash the cans well and remove the labels.
- Hammer any rough edges smooth.
- Paint the cans in bright colours – it may be necessary to use two coats of paint.
- Using the screwdriver, hammer a hole near the bottom of one of the cans. Hammer another hole opposite across from the first hole. Repeat with the other can.
- Thread nylon cord or rope through the holes of each can.
- Stand the cans upside down. In order to cut the cord to the correct length, your grandchildren will need to stand on the cans. The cord needs to reach the height of your grandchildren's hands while standing on the cans.
- Cut the cord and join the two ends firmly inside each can.

> ## 💡 Grandparent tips
> - The cord length can be adjusted to suit each stilt walker.
> - Keep the stilts stored at your place for a challenging but fun activity. Older grandchildren can make extra sets to take home and share with friends.

Skipping and jump rope

Skipping works well with chants and rhymes and also develops your grandchildren's coordination skills.

Age level: 5–12 years

Number of children: 2 or more

What you need:

- A skipping rope or a length of rope.
- A beanbag.

How to play:

- **Skipping with a partner** is the most fun and also the easiest way to learn how to skip. Two people hold each end of the skipping rope (or a longer piece of rope if the children are older), and turn the ends while someone in the middle jumps over the rope. If there are only two of you, one person can turn one end of the rope, while the other end can be tied to a fence or tree.

- After grandchildren have learned how to skip, they can move onto **skipping solo** with their own rope. Make sure it is the correct length and easy for young children to turn. There are many steps or jumps your grandchildren can learn, such as the feet-together jump and the alternate-foot jump. Older children can test their skipping prowess by counting their own number of skips, or alternating a certain number of skips at a slow pace, then at a fast pace.

- **Jumping rope** is an energetic but simple game for your grandchildren to play. Tie the beanbag to the end of the rope and swing the rope around just above the ground. Your grandchildren can jump over the rope as it comes around. If the rope makes contact with a player, they are out. The winner is the last one in. (Make sure all players take a turn at swinging the rope around.)

Hopscotch

Hopscotch is a timeless game, with plenty of variations. In all versions of hopscotch, a grid is chalked or drawn on the ground.

Age level: 5–12 years

Number of children: 1 or more

What you need:

- ✇ A hard, flat surface to play on.
- ✇ Chalk to mark lines.
- ✇ A small stone.

How to play:

- ◎ Find a level surface and draw a hopscotch grid with chalk. If it is sand or earth, mark the grid out with a stick. Each box should be about 44 cm square.
- ◎ Number each box.
- ◎ Draw a starting line 60 cm from the hopscotch grid.
- ◎ A player stands behind the starting line and throws the stone into each space in turn. They hop up and down the grid, making sure not to step on a line, and pick up the stone on the return journey.
- ◎ When two spaces are beside each other, the player may rest with both feet on the ground, one foot in each space.
- ◎ The player loses their turn if they miss the square with their stone or step on a line. The player's stone is left in the square to be repeated on their next turn.

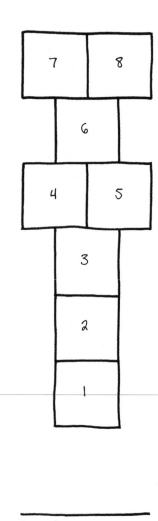

Starting line

Ball games

Age level: 5–12 years

Number of children: 2 or more

What you need:

📝 A variety of soft, medium-sized balls, balloons and light beach balls.

Throwing, catching, kicking, bouncing and dribbling balls are all skills that help children develop and improve their ball-game skills. Playing simple, small-scale versions of different games will help your grandchildren's coordination and movement skills. It will also help develop their sense of fair play and team spirit.

You can help very young grandchildren **catch a ball** successfully if they cup their hands together in front of their body. Prompt them to 'catch' the ball. Then prompt them to throw it back to you. In the beginning, stand very close to the child. Move further away as they learn how to successfully catch the ball. Give lots of cheering and encouragement.

💡 Grandparent tips

- Large balls are best for small grandchildren to use. An 18–20 cm diameter ball of foam or soft vinyl is a good size for early years.
- Small balls provide a good challenge for older children.
- Older grandchildren will enjoy a basketball ring in your garden. They can use it to improve their goal shooting or hold a competition. Who can get the most hoops out of a set number of throws?

French cricket

This is a simple bat and ball game to play using basic hitting and catching skills. There is no running by the batter and no stumps are needed.

Age level: 5–12 years

Number of children: 2 or more

What you need:

- A tennis ball.
- A cricket bat.

How to play:

- One person is chosen to bat first. The batter stands with feet together and holds the bat in front of their legs.
- Another player throws the ball underarm in an attempt to hit the batter's legs. Other players field the ball.
- The batter defends with the bat. They can hit in any direction but they are not allowed to move their feet at all – even if the throw comes from behind. Instead, they have to twist around to defend themselves.
- The ball has to be thrown from the place it lands every time.
- The batter is out if caught or if hit on the legs.
- When the batter is hit, the person who threw the ball is the next player in.

Wall tennis

There are so many ball games you can play with your grandchildren – even more if you have a wall. Wall tennis is a good example as rules are kept to a minimum.

Age level: 5–12 years

Number of children: 2 or more

What you need:
- A tennis ball.
- A wall.

How to play:
- The two players face the wall. One of the players begins by 'serving'.
- Each player must hit the ball with the flat of their hand.
- The ball must bounce once in front of the wall, then against the wall and once again on the ground before the next player hits it.
- If the player doesn't get to the ball in time, or hits it directly against the wall without bouncing, they lose the point.
- The winner of each point has the next serve.
- The game is over when one player reaches 21.

💡 **Grandparent tip**
- If you don't have a suitable wall available, check out your local park.

Tether tennis

This is a simple version of the games you can buy from toy shops. Your grandchildren will be able to enjoy plenty of hitting practice without the ball vanishing over the fence!

Age level: 5–12 years

Number of children: 2 or more

What you need:

- A tennis ball.
- Stocking or pantihose.
- A broom handle or garden stake.

How to play:

- Place a ball in the end of a stocking or pantihose and fix it to a broom handle or garden stake.
- Drive the broom handle or stake firmly into the ground.
- The player has to try to wrap the stocking around the stake by hitting the ball in one direction, while the opponent hits the ball in the opposite direction.

> ## Grandparent tip
> - This is a good game to set up for a single grandchild, providing them with plenty of hitting practice.

Skittles

Your grandchildren can have fun making their own bowling rink and then playing skittles.

Age level: 5–12 years

Number of children: 2 or more

What you need:
- 10 empty plastic drink bottles with lids (each 1 litre).
- Decorating supplies such as paint, glitter, glue and coloured paper.
- A paintbrush.
- A funnel.
- 10 cups of sand, rice or beans.
- A tennis ball.

What to do:
- Decorate the bottles and allow them to dry.
- Use the funnel to fill each bottle with a cup of sand, rice or beans.

How to play:
- Set up the skittles in various patterns, for example, four skittles in the back row, then three, then two, then one skittle.
- Grandchildren can take turns to see how many skittles they can knock down with the tennis ball. Older grandchildren can make score cards to keep score of the games they play.

⚲ Grandparent tip
- Roll the ball at the bottles to test them. If the bottles knock over too easily, add more sand. If they don't knock over easily enough, remove some sand.

Quoits

These quoits are fun to make and play.

Age level: 5–12 years

Number of children: 2 or more

What you need:

- Paper or plastic plates.
- Scissors.
- A stick.

How to play:

- Cut the centre out of the paper or plastic plates, making a ring.
- Bang a stick into the ground. You need it to stand up straight about 20 cm out of the ground.
- Each grandchild stands in a designated spot and tosses their homemade quoit in the direction of the stick.
- Points are scored each time a quoit goes over the stick.

Grandparent tip

- Show your grandchildren how to hold the quoit horizontally and to flick their wrist.

Treasure trail

An outdoor treasure trail is similar to an indoor treasure hunt (see page 17), providing plenty of excitement for energetic grandchildren. After you've laid the treasure trail, you can sit back and enjoy the fun.

Age level: 3–12 years

Number of children: 2 or more

What you need:

- Treasure – an easily hidden object such as a toy, jewellery or tin of sweets to share.
- A pen or pencil.
- 'Post-it' notes or small slips of paper.
- Paper to make the treasure map.

What to do:

- Choose a good place to hide the treasure.
- Plan your trail backwards, leaving a trail of five to ten clues written on small pieces of paper.
- Make a treasure map and include clues or instructions. For example, walk 20 paces and look behind a wormy place. (Answer: Compost bin.)
- You can involve other adults in the hunt by including them in the written clues. For example, draw a furry animal for Grandpa, and then Grandpa can give the next clue.

Grandparent tips

- Make it clear which areas of the garden are out of bounds.
- Make sure your garden is safe and hazard-proof.
- Dressing up as pirates adds to the fun.
- It's quite acceptable for grandparents to join in and help young treasure hunters read the clues.
- Grandparents can take part in the hunt if numbers are low – but they should definitely not find the treasure!

Marbles

Many grandparents will remember owning a treasured collection of marbles. Maybe some of you even still have your marble collections!

Marble ring game

Age level: 5–12 years

Number of children: 2 or more

What you need:

✎ Chalk.

✎ 8 to 10 marbles.

How to play:

◎ Draw two circles – an inner circle about 30 cm wide and an outer shooting circle 2 m wide.

◎ Each player places two or three marbles in the inner circle.

◎ The players stay outside the outer circle and take turns to shoot a marble into the inner circle. Marbles are won if they are knocked out of the inner circle by a player's 'shooter' marble.

◎ The game can be played with each player continuing until they fail to knock out a marble. Or you can play by taking turns, one shot at a time, whether you knock out a marble or not.

◎ The winner is the player with the most marbles after all the marbles have been shot from the inner circle.

⚲ Grandparent tips

- Shooting techniques need to be agreed on by players.
- It can take some time to practise shooting marbles with a flick of a thumb in order to play successfully.

Marble bombs

Age level: 5–12 years

Number of children: 2 or more

What you need:

✎ Chalk.

✎ 8 to 10 marbles.

This is an easy marble game for younger grandchildren. Make sure they don't use your treasured marbles!

How to play:

◎ Draw a circle about 30 cm wide on the ground.

◎ Each player places two or three marbles inside the circle.

◎ Each player takes turns to 'bomb' the circle with one of their marbles.

◎ The 'bomb' marble should be dropped by holding an arm outstretched at eye level above the circle. Any marbles bombed out of the circle are taken by the bomber.

◎ The game is over when there are no marbles left in the centre.

Green activities

Developing your grandchildren's awareness of our planet can be as simple as taking them for a walk in your garden in the rain and counting earthworms that have escaped from their flooded burrows. Older grandchildren will learn about the positive things they can do to sustain our planet when they make environmental projects.

Mini compost bin

Making a mini compost bin is an ongoing activity. Grandchildren can look for changes in the layers, colour, size and shape of the plant material. Is there any mould growing? Can they see any small creatures feeding on the plant material? When it's ready, the compost can be used as a plant fertiliser or soil conditioner.

Age level: 3–12 years

Number of children: 1 or more

What you need:
- A large plastic bottle.
- Gardening gloves for grandparents and grandchildren
- 2 cups of garden soil.
- A spoon.
- 2 cups of finely chopped fruit or vegetable scraps.
- 1 dessert spoon of organic fertiliser.
- 1 cup of crushed dry leaves.
- 1 cup of torn newspaper.
- Adhesive tape.

What to do:
- Cut the top from the large plastic bottle.
- Using gardening gloves and a spoon, fill the bottle. Start with a layer of soil, then fruit or vegetable scraps.

- Cover the scraps with soil, then sprinkle some fertiliser over it.
- Continue to build up layers using leaves and torn newspaper.
- Finish with a layer of soil and fertiliser.
- Spray the surface with water.
- Put the top on the bottle and secure it with tape.

Grandparent tip

- Explain to grandchildren the value of compost. It saves money, because otherwise we have to pay people to take away our waste. Composting reduces the demand for landfill sites and produces great natural fertiliser for the garden.

Wormery

A wormery provides a fascinating ongoing activity for grandchildren. Dig some up from the garden and watch for signs that worms have turned over the soil and let in essential air and water. Observing worms in the wormery will help your grandchildren to learn about the important job worms do in the natural world.

Age level: 5–12 years

Number of children: any

What you need:

- A large glass jar.
- Soil.
- Sand.
- Vegetable scraps or compost.
- Three or four worms.
- Pantihose.
- Rubber bands.
- Black plastic or paper.

What to do:

- Fill the jar three-quarters full with a layer of soil, followed by a layer of sand and then another layer of soil.
- Cover the top layer of soil with vegetable scraps or compost.
- Place the worms in the container.
- Cover the jar with pantihose and fasten with rubber bands.
- Tape some black plastic or paper around the jar to keep out the light. (Worms do not like light.)
- Sprinkle the contents of the jar with water – it needs to be moist; not soggy.
- Place the jar in a cool spot.
- Add food scraps each week.

💡 Grandparent tips

- Make sure your grandchildren return the worms to where they found them when they have finished observing them.
- Larger outdoor worm farms can be successfully developed using plastic fruit boxes stacked on top of each other.
- You can also buy commercial worm farms.

Rain gauge

Age level: 5–12 years

Number of children: 1 or more

What you need:

- A straight-sided glass jar.
- A plastic funnel.
- Waterproof insulation tape.
- A ruler.
- A waterproof felt-tip pen.

A simple rain gauge is useful for comparing how much rain falls from day to day.

What to do:

- Put the funnel inside the jar and fix it in place with the waterproof insulation tape. Because of its greater surface area, the funnel will collect more rain than the jar alone.
- Using the ruler, mark rainfall measurements on the bottle with the waterproof felt-tip pen.
- Your grandchildren can record the rain that falls each day, each week or each month. Help them to log the information on a chart.

Dream catcher

A dream catcher guarantees sweet dreams when hung up in your grandchildren's bedroom. It captures and removes bad dreams and leaves good dreams.

Age level: 8–12 years

Number of children: 1 or more

What you need:
- A flexible twig about 50 cm long.
- Thin wire.
- String, wool or cord.
- Beads, feathers and leaves.

What to do:
- Join the two ends of the twig together to make a hoop. Wrap the wire around the overlapping ends.
- Cut a few metres of string.
- Tie one end of the string to the twig hoop.
- Thread a few beads onto the string. Wrap the other end of the string around the hoop.
- Repeat a few times until you have made a web design across the hoop.
- Cut three shorter lengths of string. Tie them on the bottom of the hoop.
- String beads and tie feathers and leaves onto the end of each piece of string.
- Make a loop at the top of the dream catcher for hanging.

💡 Grandparent tip
- Grandchildren can collect feathers and leaves for their dream catcher when they are out and about with you.

Out and about

Introduction

Activities such as **backyard bird- and insect-watching** take on a new dimension when you venture into a wider, wilder environment. To get the most from the experience, it's best to plan carefully before you and your grandchildren step out into the great outdoors. Choose activities that you enjoy, and that won't test your energy levels and physical ability. For example, don't go rock-climbing if you have a dodgy knee, or take a boat on the river if you can't paddle a canoe.

Contact your local council or library for **places of interest** to visit. Check local newspapers for listings and notices of local events, concerts and performances that will interest your grandchildren. If you have a grandchild with a disability, check out the accessibility of facilities well before you start your adventure.

Hiring rather than purchasing equipment is an economical way to experience the challenge of a new **outdoor adventure**. Some other things you may find useful are:

- Backpacks to match the carrying ability of grandchildren.
- Sunhats.
- Sunscreen.
- Sensible shoes and all-weather gear.
- Food and drink.
- Pencils and notepads.
- A watch.
- A camera.

Neighbourhood map

Age level: 5–12 years

Number of children: 1 or more

What you need:

- ▨ A street map of your area.
- ▨ Paper.
- ▨ Felt-tip pens.

A neighbourhood map is a fun way for your grandchildren to become familiar with your local environment.

What to do:

- ◎ Locate your home on the map.
- ◎ Draw your local streets on the paper.
- ◎ Draw your house and add familiar landmarks such as shops and trees.
- ◎ Following the map you have drawn, take your grandchildren out and about so they can discover new streets and landmarks to add to the map.

𝒬 Grandparent tips

- Younger grandchildren can make a larger map of your area on cardboard. They can drive toy cars or walk their toys around it.
- Use public transport with your grandchildren – it is a huge adventure for children of all ages.
- Have a look on the internet for amazing websites that show a view from space of your local area.

Garage sale

Age level: 8–12 years

What you need:

- Goods to sell, such as old toys, books and ornaments.
- Cardboard and paper to make advertising signs and posters.
- Stick-on labels and pens for pricing goods.
- Tables or blankets to display items for sale.
- A cash box and change.

Hold a garage sale at your home with your grandchildren.

What to do:

- Have a good look through your cupboards, drawers, wardrobes and garage for goods you no longer need. You might find clothes, linen, books, magazines, toys and tools to sell at your garage sale.
- Place a sticker on each item and write an estimated price.
- Choose a date and time for your garage sale. Advertise in the local papers and shops and make posters for street-corner fences or posts.
- Be prepared to set up your sale at the crack of dawn. Garage-sale shoppers arrive early.
- Display your goods on tables in the garage, or in front of your house.
- Help your grandchildren when they take payments and give change.

♀ Grandparent tips

- Grandchildren can practise their bargaining skills with you, and sell things for a little less than the price marked.
- After the garage sale, donate any unsold goods to a charity shop.

Busking

Age level: 5–12 years

Number of children: any

What you need:

- A suitable location and date.
- Food and drink.
- A seat for yourself.
- A container for money.

Busking is a fun experience for your grandchildren and their audience. Many talented children enjoy the opportunity to give a street performance.

What to do:

- Check with your local council to see if you need to apply for a permit to comply with guidelines. Also check with shop owners before busking.
- Check out a few street performers to see what works well. Many performers work in set locations on weekends.
- Create engaging outfits or unusual props.
- Put aside some time for your grandchildren to rehearse and time their act with you.

Caution: When your grandchildren are in your care, busking is a 100 per cent supervision job.

Grandparent tip

- Busking can include clowning, musical performances, magic shows and 'living statues' (where a made-up mime artist poses as a statue and stands motionless).

Shopping

Age level: 3–12 years

Number of children: any

What you need:

- ✎ A little pocket money.
- ✎ Comfortable shoes.

If you are a shopping enthusiast, and love the razzle-dazzle of shopping centres, take older grandchildren shopping with you. Be warned though: some young children do not take to shopping at all well.

What to do:

- ❂ Choose a quiet time to go shopping. For instance, after school can be a disastrously crowded time.
- ❂ Avoid sales.
- ❂ Hardware, book and office supply stores can be surprisingly interesting places for older grandchildren.
- ❂ Avoid toy shops, unless you have unlimited funds.
- ❂ Don't shop for clothes that require a visit to the changing room.
- ❂ Break the boredom of shopping for necessities by visiting a pet shop, or stop for a child-friendly morning tea.

Markets are interesting places to visit with your grandchildren. Together, you can buy fresh fruit, vegetables and other produce direct from the grower.

Your grandchildren will have fun looking at the recycled toys, books, games and other items for sale at **garage sales** or markets, and they can purchase something special with their pocket money.

Shopping in **supermarkets** can be an entertaining, cooperative activity to enjoy with your grandchildren – or it can be a total disaster. Be prepared! Supermarkets are perfect places for young grandchildren to pull tantrums and tricks such as hiding or running. Flashes of uncooperative behaviour can develop between sibling grandchildren. If this happens, stop shopping and return home as soon as possible. Other **supermarket shopping hints** include:

- Provide young children with the **opportunity to help** when you're out shopping. You could give them specific tasks, such as asking them to find items for you. For example: 'Tom, can you find the yellow packet for Grandpa?', 'Where is the packet with B on it?', 'Maria, can you reach that little can with a cat on it?'
- **Plan a meal** or menu with your grandchildren. **Prepare a shopping list**, and ask your grandchildren to tick off each item from the list as you shop.
- Give older grandchildren a **calculator to tally prices** as goods are added to the trolley.

Caution: Supermarkets and car parks can be dangerous places for young grandchildren. Keep them in sight at all times.

Playing shops

Age level: 3–5 years

Number of children: any

What you need:

- A counter.
- Goods to sell – recycle used packaging and reconstruct it.
- 'Play' money. Cover cardboard disks with foil and create fake notes with felt-tip pens or pencils.
- A shopping bag.

Playing shops is an imaginative playtime activity for young grandchildren.

What to do:

Grandparents and grandchildren can take turns in being the shop keeper and customer in the make-believe shop.

Dining out

Age level: 3–12 years

Number of children: any

What you need:

- Small, healthy snacks in case dinner is delayed.
- Crayons and pencils and pad or activity book can be helpful while children wait for the meal.
- One or two books.
- Disposable wipes are handy for the occasional accident.

Dining out with your grandchildren can be an enjoyable experience, whether for breakfast, lunch, afternoon tea or dinner. It's important for children to know how to behave in a restaurant – to enjoy the experience of eating good food, but not be intimidated by the ritual of being served. Introduce older grandchildren to the pleasure of eating out by dressing up for the occasion and making it a special treat. Choose a lively, friendly restaurant or café for younger grandchildren. Other hints include:

- Find out the opening times of the restaurant you choose to visit. Make a booking, if necessary, and arrive on time. This way you can eat and leave before young grandchildren become tired or grumpy.
- Check if outdoor areas are non-smoking and if toilets are easily accessible.
- Ask if the menu caters for young grandchildren, for example, can you get a bowl of chips and a glass of apple juice?
- Take something to distract children so they can be entertained quietly while you wait.

Picnics

Age level: 3–12 years

Number of children: any

What you need:

- Bread and butter knives.
- A knife or cutters in different shapes, for example, you could cut the sandwiches into animal shapes.
- A chopping board.
- A fork for mashing.
- A small bowl.
- A grater.
- Sliced bread, bread rolls, flat bread for making wraps or pita pockets that you can stuff.
- Butter or margarine.
- Fillings of your choice.

Picnicking outdoors can be as simple as enjoying a meal in your garden or local park, or it can be a major excursion to a spectacular picnic spot. You can pack a picnic hamper, or each grandchild can carry their own food and drink in their backpacks.

Picnics are an excellent way of eliminating stress from meal times, but they need **careful planning**. Make finger-sized sandwiches, pies and cakes that everyone will enjoy. Take along plastic bottles of frozen water to keep food cool, and pack some fruit and bottles of juice to drink.

Thinking green and being garbage-free means using fabric rather than disposable napkins. It means bringing along your own food containers, cutlery and crockery that can be taken home and washed, ready to be re-used.

Sandwiches are excellent for picnics and excursions. You can shop for the ingredients together, then show your grandchildren how to prepare their favourite sandwiches. Begin by using their favourite fillings, and then introduce different combinations. Older children with good appetites can make double-decker and even triple-decker sandwiches. Suggestions for fillings include:

- Honey and mashed banana.
- Cream cheese and raisins.
- Tuna mixed with mayonnaise and sweet corn.
- Mashed hard-boiled egg, plain or mixed with mayonnaise.
- Chicken and yoghurt.
- Sliced salami and tomato.
- Chopped ham or chicken mixed with pineapple chunks and mayonnaise.
- Peanut butter and grated apple.
- Peanut butter with or without jam.
- Vegemite sprinkled with grated cheese.
- Chopped celery and grated carrot mixed with cottage cheese and natural yoghurt.
- Lettuce, tomato and other salad ingredients.

Grandparent tips

- Don't forget to bring a waterproof picnic rug.
- If the thought of mud and ants is alarming, lightweight tables and chairs are a comforting alternative.

Cycling

Age level: 5–12 years

Number of children: any

What you need:

- Bicycle.
- Helmet, sunscreen and all-weather gear.
- Drink bottle.

Cycling is a healthy recreation to share with your grandchildren. If you haven't ridden a bicycle for some time, get some **practice** before you set out on a cycling expedition together. When you go cycling with your grandchildren – whether they are riding 2- or 3-wheeled bicycles – be sure that they understand the **responsibility** connected with safe cycling.

When **planning a cycling trip**, choose a suitable route following cycle paths. Keep an eye on how far you have travelled – don't forget to factor in the return journey. Remember to take drinks and snacks along and wear sunscreen and all-weather gear.

Bicycles themselves are not dangerous. It is the inability to control them, and to follow simple road rules, that can lead to accidents and injuries. Other **safety tips** include:

- Always wear a helmet.
- Familiarise yourself with current road-safety rules.
- Check that the brakes are working.
- Ride on cycle paths or quiet streets.
- Always supervise children when riding on roads – even quiet roads.
- Keep to the correct side of the road.
- Look out for pedestrians, other cyclists and approaching cars.
- Use hand signals to indicate your intention before making a turn.
- When not making signals, keep both hands on the handlebars and feet on the pedals at all times.

- Wear bright clothes so motorists and pedestrians can see you easily.
- Stay alert and watch out for animals, posts, gutters, sharp corners, bumps, holes in the ground and slippery and loose surfaces.

Helmets

Helmets are the most important accessory for cycling. All cyclists, regardless of age, must wear a Standards Australia–approved bicycle helmet whenever they ride.

- Choose a helmet for your grandchild that fits well and is comfortable.
- An unsuitable helmet will not give proper protection. It should not move backwards or forwards, and not move forwards over the eyes.
- The helmet should be well ventilated and not too heavy for children.

> ### Grandparent tip
> - Always check with parents before giving your grandchildren a bicycle.

Caring for the planet

Your grandchildren can learn to care for the planet by using the four R's: Rethink, Reduce, Reuse and Recycle. Try some of the following **planet-saving ideas**.

- Save energy and reduce pollution by walking, cycling and using public transport whenever possible.
- Save energy. Switch off lights and turn off heaters, the TV and computers at the wall when they are not being used.
- Wear an extra layer of warm clothing rather than turning on the heater.
- Wear cool, light clothing rather than using the air-conditioner.
- Use water wisely. Help your grandchildren to understand that water is our most precious resource. Encourage them to conserve it by taking short showers and by not leaving a tap running – ever.
- Recycle cans, waste paper and bottles.
- Buy products that are packaged in (or even made of) recycled material.
- Avoid buying over-packaged goods.
- Recycle clothes, old toys, books and games by giving them to someone else or to a charity shop.
- Compost food scraps.
- Don't drop litter.
- Write on both sides of a piece of paper. Make scribble pads from recycled paper.

Clean-up day

Encourage your grandchildren to care for the planet by recruiting them to work with you to clean up your street, local park or area.

Age level: 5–12 years

Number of children: any

What you need:

☑ Old clothes for grandchildren to wear.

☑ Strong gloves.

☑ Bags to collect litter.

☑ Food tongs.

What to do:

⚙ Choose a local area that needs cleaning.

⚙ Wearing old clothes and gloves, your grandchildren can use food tongs to fill garbage bags with rubbish.

💡 Grandparent tips

- You can also join community action groups that protect, support and conserve the local environment. Involve your grandchildren and their families in events such as local clean-up days.
- Grandchildren can take part in campaigns to make people aware of endangered animals or plants, and schemes such as Adopt-a-Local-Stream.

Excursions

Excursions can help develop your grandchildren's interests. You could attend the ballet or an air show, for example, watch a horse gymkhana, a puppet or magic show or visit a vintage car collection. Or you could introduce your grandchildren to a pastime that you particularly enjoy, for example, go to the cinema, theatre, a concert or art gallery you're fond of visiting.

If you love **live theatre**, you can share this exciting experience with your grandchildren, whether it's a play, ballet, opera or pop concert. Children of about five or six should be ready to attend a live performance. Watch out for local performances at halls or shopping malls or your local children's theatre.

For your grandchildren's first experience of live theatre, select a performance that specially caters for youngsters. Before you attend a performance, give your grandchildren some idea of the plot or what to expect and explain the protocol of live theatre. For example, you mustn't talk during a performance because the actors are putting on a special show for the audience.

With their wide screens and massed seating, **cinemas** offer quite a different experience from viewing DVDs at home. Again, you may need to explain ahead of time that you mustn't talk during the screening. You need to keep up to date with viewing ratings, and research reviews when selecting a film that is suitable for your grandchildren. Allow time after the film to talk about it with your grandchildren.

A **small exhibition** by a single painter may be a good way to introduce grandchildren to the joy of viewing art. Many **art galleries** operate workshops and activities for children during holidays. To make it fun:

- Find the paintings, displays or objects that children can relate to.
- Ask your grandchildren to choose their favourite artwork. Talk about what you both like about it. Can they make up their own title for it?
- Talk about the people depicted in the paintings. What do you think they are thinking about?
- Play 'I spy' using objects in the painting.

Most children put **theme parks and zoos or animal sanctuaries** at the top of their list of favourite excursions. Many of these attractions have special trails and holiday programmes specifically designed for children. Take advantage of the picnic areas, shelters and barbecues – and don't forget to find out about animal feeding times.

Most **museums** have child-friendly exhibits and hands-on activities. Check out times, entrance prices and how to get there to ensure hassle-free visits.

Living museums and National Trust **historic towns and properties** allow grandchildren to experience and imagine what life would be like if they were zapped back into the past. Many historic homes have child-friendly exhibits and activities.

☝ Grandparent tips

- Don't forget inexpensive excursion options such as picnics, walks and exploring local parks and gardens.
- Pack snacks, sandwiches and drinks to take on excursions, so impromptu picnics can be held at any time.
- Waiting in queues is tiring for young children – and grandparents – so booking tickets in advance takes the hassle from attending events or performances.
- Choose your seats carefully so your grandchildren can see the action. Aisle seats are good if you need to make a quick escape.
- Use folded coats or pack inflatable cushions to help young grandchildren have a better view.
- Take drinks and snacks along for the interval breaks, to avoid having to wait in queues. You might need to use that time for a toilet break.

Popcorn

Popcorn is a great portable snack to take along for your grandchildren to snack on when you go on an excursion.

Age level: 5–12 years

Number of children: any

What you need:

- Measuring cups and spoons.
- A large saucepan with a tight-fitting lid.
- A large serving bowl.
- A sieve.

Ingredients:

2 tablespoons oil
½ cup uncooked popcorn
salt or icing sugar

What to do:

- Place the oil and popcorn in a large saucepan and cover with a lid.
- Place on the stove over a high heat.
- Shake the pan to settle the popcorn evenly in the oil.
- The corn will start to pop when the oil is hot enough, and it will stop popping when it is cooked.
- Tip the cooked popcorn into a large serving bowl. You can serve it plain, with salt, or with a light dusting of icing sugar using a sieve.
- Take in a sealed container or individual paper bags.

Grandparent tips

- Keep the lid on the saucepan or the popcorn will pop all over kitchen!
- Store any plain, uneaten cooked popcorn in an airtight container.

Watching sports events

Grandparents often help out with ferrying grandchildren to play team sports, and are frequently invited to watch their grandchildren play. Grandchildren in turn will be happy to accompany you when you go along to support your own favourite team.

It is vital that grandparents model the best spectator behaviour – whether you are watching your grandchildren in their sporting activities or sharing your favourite spectator sport with them. At all times support:

- Fair play.
- The rules of the game.
- Decisions of umpires and officials.

♀ Grandparent tips

- Congratulate your grandchildren whether they win, lose or draw.
- Take along a portable chair or stool, a waterproof picnic rug and an umbrella, whether it is hot or cold.
- Include something to read or do if it is going to be a long day, such as when grandchildren play in district competitions.
- Make sure to take a thermos of tea or coffee and a snack.

Team streamers

Streamers made in team colours are easy to make. Your grandchildren can take them along to sports events and cheer on their teams.

Age level: 5–12 years

Number of children: 1 or more

What you need:
- Crepe paper in team colours.
- Scissors.
- Strong glue or tape.
- A ruler or a piece of dowel for the streamer wand.

What to do:
- Cut out lengths of crepe paper.
- Choose strips in team colours and glue them to the end of the ruler or piece of dowel.
- Roll the streamers around the wand tightly and then unwind.
- Show your grandchildren how to wave the streamers to cheer on their team.

Exploring

Exploring a 'wild' place where your grandchildren can safely enjoy being outdoors is a fun activity. It's a good idea to select a park that will suit your grandchildren's ages.

Local parks with playgrounds are perfect places where young grandchildren can burn up energy. Parks with lakes and ponds will delight them, with birds to be fed and closely studied. Parks with paths and tracks suitable for bikes and small treks are also ideal. While visiting the local park is an exciting experience for young grandchildren, it is perhaps not so special for older children. They might enjoy following unmade paths and spaces with trees and undergrowth to add excitement to their explorations.

National parks offer grandchildren opportunities to explore a variety of activities such as bushwalking, picnicking, camping, canoeing and wildlife watching.

Check out the facilities at the park before you visit. Most national parks provide shelters if the weather turns ugly. Parks with outdoor cooking facilities provide a challenging and fun change from cooking and dining at home.

 Grandparent tip

- Individual bottles of water are vital if excursions take you and your grandchildren away from a source of water.

Bark and leaf rubbings

A trip to a park to make bark or leaf rubbings is an interesting way for grandchildren to discover different types of trees.

Age level: 5–12 years

Number of children: any

What you need:

- Sheets of strong paper.
- Sticky tape.
- Crayons or pastels.

What to do:

- **To make a bark rubbing,** choose a tree with an interesting bark pattern. Tape a piece of paper to the tree.
- Using even strokes, rub a crayon or pastel on the paper. Keep the paper pressed flat against the trunk of the tree so it doesn't tear or move.
- Make various bark rubbings with different coloured crayons or pastels.
- **To make a leaf rubbing,** place a sheet of paper over a leaf with the veins facing up.
- Keep the paper still and rub over where you can feel the leaf.

Grandparent tips

- A bark rubbing works best when the tree trunk is dry.
- Grandchildren can make a collection of their bark and leaf rubbings by pasting them into a scrapbook and labelling them with the name, date and location.
- Help your grandchildren to identify trees and plants by borrowing books from the library or researching the topic on the internet.

Nature weaving

Your grandchildren can collect natural materials to weave when they are out and about. The activity will increase their awareness of different textures in nature.

Age level: 8–12 years

Number of children: any

What you need:
- 12-ply wool.
- Scissors.
- Two sticks or branches about 60 cm long.
- A ruler.
- Adhesive tape.
- A collection of grasses, leaves, bark, seed pods, feathers, twigs and other suitable materials.
- Natural dyed wool scraps to weave with other natural materials.

What to do:
- Measure and cut pieces of wool approximately 40 cm long.
- Tie each piece of wool to one of the sticks to form the top of the frame. Using a ruler, space each strand of wool approximately 3 cm apart. To form the bottom of the frame, tie each piece of wool to the other stick, similarly evenly spaced.
- Run a strip of adhesive tape along the length of each stick or branch to stop the wool slipping while weaving.
- To support the frame, tie a piece of wool to each end of the top stick or branch. Hang it from a suitable object such as a door handle or hook.
- Begin weaving the collection of natural materials between the vertical strands of wool. Weave interesting patterns.

♀ Grandparent tip
- The weave will look best if your grandchildren do not leave large gaps in their weavings.

Scroggin

Scroggin is a traditional, sustaining snack food for walkers. Your grandchildren can help you make it and pack it in their backpacks when they go adventuring and exploring with you.

Age level: 5–12 years

Number of children: any

What you need:
- Measuring cups and spoons.
- A bowl.
- Scissors.
- A knife.
- A chopping board.
- Large sealed container.

Ingredients:

2 tablespoons sunflower seeds

½ cup sultanas

½ cup raisins

12 dried figs or apricots, cut into quarters

½ cup peanuts

½ cup almonds

100 g chopped chocolate or chocolate chips (optional)

What to do:
- Mix the sunflower seeds with the dried fruit in a bowl, then add the nuts and chocolate (if using).
- Place in a sealed container and shake vigorously.

Grandparent tip
- Scroggin doesn't keep for long, as the nuts tend to go soft.

Wildlife-watching

Wildlife-watching with young grandchildren can be as simple as going to the park and feeding the ducks. Older grandchildren can keep records of the wildlife they observe in the environment.

Age level: 3–12 years

Number of children: any

What you need:
- Sunhat.
- Sunscreen.
- Sensible shoes and protective clothing.
- Backpacks.
- Food and drink.
- A notepad and pencil.
- A watch.
- Tweezers, a magnifying glass and plastic containers (with lids punched with air holes) for collecting and observing plants and small creatures.
- Binoculars for observing birds.

To **protect the wildlife**, keep the following in mind.

- Pass the Explorer's Code on to your grandchildren: observe, explore, enjoy, protect and conserve wildlife and its habitat.
- Tread carefully and watch the ground as you walk. Respect even the smallest creatures and take care not to destroy their homes.
- Avoid touching living things with your hands. Do not put fingers into holes or places you can't see into. If you're not sure what will happen if you pick up a mini-sized creature, leave it alone.
- Do not interfere with bird's nests. Touching a bird's nest can result in the parent bird abandoning it altogether.

Nature diary

Your grandchildren can keep a nature diary and write down their observations. They can include sketches and records of the dates and times they observed plants and animals.

Age level: 5–12 years

Number of children: any

What you need:
- Pens and pencils.
- A small sketchpad.

What to do:
Children can become nature detectives as they check for tracks and trails left by day and night-time visitors.

During the day, look in the garden, in the street and in the park. Some trails will be obvious, such as a snail's trail or a dog's track in the mud. Look for unusual tracks in reference books or on the internet. Other places to look include:

- Under bark, rocks and in rotting leaf litter.
- In grass and on leaves.
- In cracks and crevices.
- In water.
- In trees.
- Flying free in the air.
- In the ground.

Adventuring at night, armed with a torch, provides exciting exploration opportunities for children. They can spotlight possums, owls, spiders, moths and other animals that come out at night for food. The early evening is a great time to watch for birds.

Your grandchildren will like to know the names of plants and animals. Use the internet or take a trip to your local library to **identify plants and animals**. Or you could invest in a collection of reference books that cover your local area.

Insect watching

Insect watching is a satisfying out-and-about activity for grandchildren of all ages. There are always plenty of insects and bugs to observe. Encourage younger children to look for nibbled leaves, to count the spots on the back of a ladybird, to listen and to draw the insects they observe.

Age level: 3–12 years

Number of children: any

What you need:

- Magnifying glass.

What to look for:

- Insect eggs.
- Cocoons and caterpillars.
- Butterflies and moths.
- Ants and bees.
- Slugs and snails.
- Flies, aphids, ladybirds, grasshoppers, cockroaches, beetles, centipedes and millipedes, bugs, dragonflies and damselflies.

Grandparent tip

- In just one square metre of your garden there are probably between 500 and 2000 insects.

Insect catcher

Grandchildren will find it easy to catch and observe insects when they make this simple insect catcher using a drinking straw. It's also called a pooter.

Age level: 5–12 years

Number of children: 1 or more

What you need:

- A piece of stocking or pantihose.
- A drinking straw cut in half and split at one end.
- Sticky tape.
- A glass jar with a lid.

What to do:

- Place the piece of stocking or pantihose over the split end of the drinking straw.
- Push one half of the straw inside the other half.
- Tape the two ends of the straw together.

Catching insects

- Place one end of the insect catcher over a mini beast. Suck lightly through the other end of the pooter. The piece of stocking or pantihose will prevent grandchildren from swallowing the insect.
- Quickly turn the insect catcher upside down and tap the insect into the jar to observe it.
- After your grandchildren have studied their insect, remind them to put it back where they found it.

Caution: Do not touch scorpions, spiders, bees, wasps, centipedes or large ants. These creatures may be poisonous if they bite or sting.

⚲ Grandparent tip
- It's important to remind your grandchildren of the importance of respecting wildlife and returning creatures to their original location.

Insect-collecting bag

An insect-collecting bag is a handy piece of equipment for grandchildren to carry with them when you are trekking outdoors.

Age level: 5–12 years

Number of children: any

What you need:

- A wire coat hanger.
- A plastic bag.
- Sticky tape.
- A plastic box or jar with air holes pierced into the lid.

What to do:

- Bend a coat hanger into a circle that's the same size as the mouth of the plastic bag.
- Tape the bag to the frame and twist the hook to make a handle.
- Take the bag outside and slowly sweep it through long grass or pat it against a hedge.
- Put any insects or bugs your grandchildren want to examine into the plastic box or jar.
- Only keep an insect long enough to observe, draw or photograph it.
- Remind your grandchildren to put the insect back where they found it.

Growing a butterfly

Observing a caterpillar until it turns into a butterfly or moth is a fascinating activity for grandchildren.

Age level: 5–12 years

Number of children: any

What you need:

- Kitchen paper towel.
- A large plastic container or wide jar.
- A piece of muslin to cover the top of the container or jar.
- A large rubber band or some masking tape.

What to do:

- Dampen the paper towel and use it to line the container or jar.
- Venture into the wilds of your garden or park to find a caterpillar.
- Your grandchildren will need to collect twigs, leaves and plant material from the caterpillar's environment.
- Using twigs or leaves carefully put the caterpillar into the container or jar, along with the plant material your grandchildren have collected. Don't touch the caterpillar now that it's safely in the jar.
- Cover the container or jar with muslin and secure it with a rubber band or tape.
- Keep replacing the plant material. It must come from where you found the caterpillar.
- Keep the caterpillar in a sheltered spot or inside at a constant temperature.
- Watch carefully as the caterpillar turns into a cocoon. Your grandchildren may be lucky enough to see the dry cocoon split and a beautiful butterfly or moth emerge.
- Let the butterfly go at once, as they have short lives. They need to fly and be free.

Ponding

Ponding is a great – but damp – activity to do with grandchildren. They can make a small net or ponding scoop to collect aquatic insects to observe. To make your own ponding scoop, attach a kitchen strainer to a long pole with cord or string. You're ready to go ponding!

Age level: 5–12 years

Number of children: 1 or more

What you need:
- Spare clothing and waterproof boots.
- A small net or ponding scoop.
- A flat plastic tray.
- A microscope or magnifying glass.

What to do:
- Dip or drag your net or ponding scoop through the waterweeds.
- Collect your catch in a flat plastic tray filled with a little water to observe the insects.
- After your grandchildren have observed the aquatic insects, return them to the pond.

⑨ Grandparent tip
- Grandchildren can observe the life cycle of frogs – from egg to tadpole to frog – when they go ponding regularly.

Frog in the pond

Frog in the pond is a special dessert for very young and not-so-young grandchildren to make and enjoy.

Age level: 5–12 years

Number of children: any

What you need:

- Two bowls.
- A spoon.
- One packet of green jelly crystals.
- Chocolate frogs.

What to do:

- Make the jelly in one of the bowls according to the instructions on the packet.
- Let the jelly cool, but not set.
- Put the chocolate frogs in the bottom of the other bowl.
- Pour the cool jelly over the frogs.
- Put the bowl in the refrigerator to set.

⚲ Grandparent tip

- Grandchildren can also make a number of smaller bowls with a frog in each serve.

Bird-watching

Bird watchers need to watch and listen quietly, so this can be a tricky activity for younger grandchildren. For older children, it could be the start of a lifelong fascination with birds.

Age level: 5–12 years

Number of children: any

What you need:
- ☞ Backpacks.
- ☞ Protective clothing.
- ☞ A notepad and pen.
- ☞ Food and drink.
- ☞ Binoculars.
- ☞ A bird field book.

What to do:
- ☼ Watch the birds in your garden, park or area.
- ☼ Wear protective clothing and pack your binoculars (see page 214), food and drink, notepad and pen in your backpack.
- ☼ Find a quiet spot and watch out for birds.
- ☼ Draw the birds in your notepad.
- ☼ Record when, where and what time you saw the birds. What were they doing?

☺ Grandparent tips
- Early-morning bird watching is a fun activity to do with early-rising grandchildren. Why not have breakfast with the birds?
- Watching the behaviour of common birds such as sparrows, starlings, pigeons and seagulls is an excellent way to introduce grandchildren to bird watching.
- Older grandchildren can use bird field books to identify the birds they observe.

Bird feeder

Make a bird feeder with your grandchildren and hang it outside a window in your home.

Age level: 3–12 years

Number of children: 1 or more

What you need:

- A clean milk or juice carton with lid screwed on tight.
- Scissors.
- String.

What to do:

- Cut a piece from the carton as shown in the diagram.
- Make a hole through the top of the lid. Thread the string through the hole and tie underneath. Reattach to the carton.
- Fill the feeder with the appropriate food for birds in your area and hang it up.
- Don't hang the feeder where cats can get at the birds. Use a high branch or a nail on the wall.

Birdbath

Age level: 3–12 years

Number of children: 1 or more

What you need:

✎ An old plastic bowl.

Fill an old plastic bowl and put it outside – out of the reach of cats. Birds will drink from the bowl and splash around in the water.

💡 **Grandparent tip**

- Bird feeders and birdbaths attract birds and provide easy bird-watching experiences for grandchildren.

Homemade binoculars

Binoculars are fun for young grandchildren to make but not as effective as real ones!

Age level: 3–8 years

Number of children: any

What you need:
- Two cardboard tubes of equal length.
- Paint and paintbrush.
- Glue.
- String.
- Scissors.
- Sticky tape.

What to do:
- Paint the cardboard tubes and let them dry.
- Glue the tubes together, side by side.
- Fasten string at the sides with sticky tape so the binoculars can hang around your grandchildren's necks.
- Be a bird detective: birds with bits of grass or straw in their beaks could be nesting. Birds with snails, worms or dragonflies in their beaks could be on their way to feed their babies.
- You can help your grandchildren to locate a bird by asking them to imagine a tree to be a clock face. For example, 'There's a vulture at the three o'clock position.'

Pancakes

Pancakes are a popular and versatile food for grandchildren, especially if they're up early to watch the birds. Leftover pancakes freeze and reheat well, too.

Age level: 3–12 years

Number of children: any

What you need:
- ✇ Measuring cups and spoons.
- ✇ A sifter or sieve.
- ✇ A medium-sized mixing bowl.
- ✇ A wooden spoon or whisk.
- ✇ A jug.
- ✇ A non-stick 20 cm frying pan.
- ✇ An egg lifter.
- ✇ A plate.
- ✇ An oven tray.

Ingredients:
1 cup plain flour
¼ teaspoon salt
1 egg
1¼ cups milk
2 tablespoons oil (if you are not using a non-stick frying pan)
lemon juice
sugar

What to do:
- ◉ Sift the flour and salt into a mixing bowl.
- ◉ Add the egg and gradually whisk or stir the milk into the flour mixture until it becomes smooth. Pour the mixture into a jug.
- ◉ Heat a frying pan. Add oil if you are using an ordinary frying pan.

- ✿ Pour about half a cup of batter into the hot pan.
- ✿ Quickly tilt the pan in all directions until a thin layer of batter covers the pan. Cook for 1 minute or until bubbles come to the surface and break.
- ✿ Carefully turn the pancake over or, to toss, slide the pancake to the far side of the frying pan. Hold the handle with both hands and flick upwards. The pancake should come down with the underside up as you catch it in the pan.
- ✿ Cook for another minute. The pancake should be golden brown on both sides.
- ✿ Slip the pancake onto a warm plate.
- ✿ Sprinkle the pancake with lemon juice and sugar, then roll it up.
- ✿ Eat the pancake immediately or put it on a tray and leave it in a warm oven while you continue cooking.
- ✿ Keep making pancakes until the batter is finished. Enjoy!

💡 Grandparent tips

Other serving suggestions include:

- Top unrolled pancakes with fruit and yoghurt or ice cream.
- Spread them with butter and top with jam or honey.
- Mix grated cheese and cooked spinach together and place it in the centre of the pancake. Roll up the pancake, add some grated cheese on top and heat it in the oven.

French toast

French toast also makes a delicious breakfast treat for early risers.

Age level: 3–12 years

Number of children: any

What you need:
- ✍ A shallow dish.
- ✍ Measuring cups and spoons.
- ✍ A fork or wire whisk.
- ✍ A knife.
- ✍ A frying pan.
- ✍ A plate.
- ✍ Foil.

Ingredients:

1 egg
½ cup milk
½ teaspoon vanilla essence or extract
2 thick slices of day-old bread
30 g butter
cinnamon and sugar or maple syrup to serve

What to do:
- ✿ Break the egg into a shallow dish.
- ✿ Add milk and vanilla essence.
- ✿ Beat with a fork or whisk until well mixed.
- ✿ Cut the bread into triangles.
- ✿ Melt half the butter in a frying pan.
- ✿ When the butter begins to bubble, dip a slice of the bread into the egg mixture, let the excess run off, and place the bread in the pan. (Do this quickly!)
- ✿ Fry the bread until it is golden brown.

⊛ Transfer the French toast to a warm plate and cover it with foil.

⊛ Add more butter to the pan and cook the remaining bread.

⊛ Serve lightly sprinkled with cinnamon and sugar or drizzled with maple syrup.

⦿ Grandparent tip

- Some grandchildren will enjoy French toast as a savoury dish served with tomatoes and bacon, or with tomato sauce.

Camping

Many grandparents are experienced campers and enjoy camping with grandchildren. However camping with grandchildren needs planning. Choose a camping site with care and make lots of lists for shelter, equipment, clothing, essentials, cooking and odds and ends to take with you.

Age level: 5–12 years

Number of children: any

What you need:

- tent and poles
- equipment – mattresses, sleeping bags, tables and chairs, stove and cooking utensils, cleaning materials
- essentials such as towels, biodegradable soap etc.
- food
- medical kit, stuff to do if it is raining, etc
- clothing. (Individual lists for grandchildren and grandparents.)

When you and your grandchildren visit a natural environment, it is your responsibility to leave it in an undisturbed condition. Don't forget to:

- Carry your rubbish out.
- Leave your campsite as you found it. The only sign of your visit should be the flattened grass where your tent stood.
- Guard against all risk of bushfire. If you use a campfire, return stones to where you found them, scatter the ash and disperse the firewood.
- Keep all lakes, rivers and creeks free of polluting agents. Use only biodegradable soap – never detergents.
- Human waste should be buried well away from campsites, water sources and tracks. Toilet paper must be burned.
- Leave pets at home.
- Keep to made tracks when bushwalking.

Useful knots

Age level: 8–12 years

Number of children: any

What you need:

📝 A rope.

Being able to tie basic knots is important when you go camping. You can teach your grandchildren these basic knots and pass on this useful skill. Older grandchildren can practise tying knots over and over so when they go camping they can tie them in the dark. Try the following knots:

- **Granny knot:** Your grandchildren will use this knot a lot, although it is not a strong knot.

- **Reef knot:** Your grandchildren can use this knot to join two pieces of the same thickness – right over left, left over right.

- **Two half hitches:** This very handy knot can be used to secure one end of a rope to a tall post or pole.

- **A sheepshank:** This is the best knot for shortening a rope without cutting it. It's useful to use if one of the guy ropes on a tent happens to be too long.

Campsite cooking

Practise cooking a few camping meals at home before setting out into the wild.

Age level: 5–12 years

Number of children: any

What you need:

☞ There is a wide range of outdoor cooking gear available, but you need to be familiar with how the equipment works before you reach your camping site.

Cooking hints

🖑 Plan meals with your grandchildren for each day. Buy supplies with care before you set out on your camping trip. Estimate that grandchildren will eat twice as much when camping as when at home.

🖑 Check fire regulations. Open campfires are banned at many camping sites and especially in certain seasons.

🖑 Make sure supplies are kept in secure containers to prevent ants and other small creatures from invading them.

🖑 Be careful with drinking water. Boil river water before drinking it or using it for cooking.

🖑 Supervise young grandchildren at all times around a barbecue or campfire.

🖑 Take care with lighting fluids, hot plates and spitting oils and fats when cooking.

Chocolate bananas

Bananas and chocolate make a great combination when the banana is wrapped in foil and cooked.

Age level: 3–12 years

Number of children: any

What you need:
- A knife.
- Foil.

Ingredients:
1 banana for each person
1 block of chocolate, cut into small pieces

What to do:
- Carefully slit the banana open, leaving the skin on.
- Slice the banana and fill it with small bits of chocolate.
- Close the banana and wrap it firmly in foil.
- Cook on a barbecue, the coals of a campfire or in an oven for 10 minutes.

Toasted marshmallows

Cooking marshmallows on a stick or toasting fork is always popular.

Age level: 3–12 years

Number of children: any

What you need:

✎ Toasting forks or a long green stick.

Ingredients:

Marshmallows

What to do:

◉ Slide a marshmallow onto a toasting fork or stick.

◉ Hold the fork over the coals for one or two minutes until it bubbles and browns.

◉ Be careful when you eat the marshmallow, as it will be hot.

Fruit dessert

This is a delicious dessert when cooked in a parcel of foil over a campfire or on a barbecue.

Age level: 3–12 years

Number of children: any

What you need:

- A vegetable peeler.
- A knife.
- Cooking foil.
- A teaspoon.
- Bowls.

Ingredients:

a piece of fruit for each person (for example, a banana, apple or pear)
butter or margarine
honey
vanilla ice cream or yoghurt (if possible to have)

What to do:

- Peel and roughly chop the fruit.
- Place the fruit, a teaspoon of butter or margarine and some honey on a sheet of foil.
- Wrap the foil around the fruit to make a parcel.
- Cook the parcel on a barbecue or campfire coals for five minutes.
- Carefully unwrap the foil parcel.
- Tip the fruit into a bowl and serve with ice cream or yoghurt.

Damper

Your grandchildren will enjoy eating these pioneer versions of bread.

Age level: 3–12 years

Number of children: any

What you need:
- A bowl.
- A cup.
- A flat tin plate.
- Cooking foil.
- A knife.

Ingredients:

2 cups self-raising flour

pinch of salt

water

dried fruit such as raisins (optional)

margarine

honey or jam

What to do:
- Mix the flour, salt and enough water to make a stiff dough.
- Add a handful of dried fruit.
- Grease a flat tin plate with margarine.
- Place the dough on the plate and cover with foil.
- Place on a barbecue or in the hot ashes of a campfire.
- It should be cooked after 60 minutes.
- To serve, cut into thick slices and spread with margarine and honey or jam.

⚲ Grandparent tip
- If the knife comes out dry and free of crumbs, the damper is ready to eat.

Twisty damper

A new twist on old-fashioned damper recipe.

Age level: 3–12 years

Number of children: any

What you need:

- A 2–3 cm diameter stick for each person.

What to do:

- Mix the dough as for the damper recipe.
- Roll balls of dough into long snakes. Coil the dough around the stick.
- Place the twisty damper on a barbecue or the coals of the campfire, turning occasionally.
- The twisty damper will pull off the stick easily when it is cooked.
- To serve, fill the hole in the middle of the twisty damper with honey or jam.

Baked potatoes

Age level: 3–12 years

Number of children: any

What you need:

- A fork.
- A sharp knife.

Baked potatoes are a sure-fire favourite for grandchildren of all ages.

Ingredients:

1 large potato for each person
fillings such as butter, cheese or mashed avocado

What to do:

- Scrub the potatoes to remove all dirt, leaving the skin (or jacket) on.
- Pierce the potatoes with a fork.
- Wrap the potatoes in foil and bake the potatoes in the coals of your campfire for 1–1¼ hours. The potatoes will be ready when you test them with a fork and they feel soft inside.
- Cut a large cross into the top of each potato.
- Give each potato a gentle squeeze so the jacket opens slightly.
- Serve the potatoes with butter or the toppings of your choice.

Hamburgers

Homemade hamburgers are excellent camping food, and easy to cook on a barbecue.

Age level: 3–12 years

Number of children: 2

What you need:

- A mixing bowl.
- Measuring cups and spoons.
- A fork or whisk.
- A spatula.
- A knife.

Ingredients:

350 g lean minced meat (beef, pork, chicken or lamb)
1 onion, finely chopped
1 egg, lightly beaten
1 cup fresh breadcrumbs
2 tablespoons tomato sauce
flour
2–4 tablespoons oil
salt and pepper
2 hamburger buns
shredded lettuce
1–2 tomatoes, sliced

What to do:

- Place the meat, onion, egg, breadcrumbs and tomato sauce in a mixing bowl.
- Mix together until well combined.
- Divide the mixture into two portions and shape into round patties.
- Roll the hamburgers in flour.

⊛ Heat the oil on the barbecue hot plate.

⊛ Cook the hamburgers for about 4–5 minutes on each side.

⊛ Cut the hamburger buns in half.

⊛ Place the bottom of the bun on a serving plate and top with lettuce and tomato, followed by the hamburger.

⊛ Add some tomato sauce and the top of the hamburger bun.

☀ Grandparent tip

- Add different ingredients, such as pineapple rings, fried onions, fried eggs, bacon or cheese slices, to suit your grandchildren's tastes.

Fishing

Age level: 5–12 years

Number of children: any

What you need:

- ✇ Rods and reels.
- ✇ Bait.
- ✇ Food and drink.
- ✇ Hats and sunscreen.
- ✇ Suitable clothing. Be prepared for hot and sunny, cold and wet weather.

Grandparents who are fervent fishing fanatics will already know what a great activity this is to enjoy with their grandchildren. Demonstrate **basic fishing skills**, such as how to cast. Don't forget to take a camera to record your catches.

The key to ensuring a successful fishing trip, rather than a fishing flop, is **careful planning**. Involve your grandchildren from the early planning stages and give them areas of responsibility, such as being in charge of food.

Select a **safe yet practical fishing spot** that takes into account the age and skills of your grandchildren. Ask your fishing friends for spots that should have suitable fish to catch and one that is easy to reach.

Estuaries where fresh and saltwater tides merge, bays and lakes are **good places to take children fishing**. Fish tend to be found near structures that offer food and protection from bigger fish such as jetties, rock walls, sunken logs, weed beds and reefs.

Basic **fishing tackle** should include floats, a few sinkers, lures and a small knife stored in a tray. Small, clear-lidded containers for storing hooks, swivels and sinkers will provide safe access. Choose tackle boxes that you and your grandchildren can carry.

Gathering **bait** can be fun. Gathering bait could be the best part of a fishing trip for your grandchildren. The ideal bait occurs naturally in the area being fished. Use a fine mesh net, a bait pump or a spade to gather bait.

Casting keeps grandchildren involved and interested when nibbles are far apart. Concentrate on accuracy rather than distance when teaching your grandchildren how to cast. A double-handed casting method is good for young anglers. Another helpful hint is to tell your grandchildren to watch the spot they are aiming for. Make sure they are balanced and comfortable to prevent any falls into the water. Avoid crowds of anglers so your grandchildren's lines don't get tangled when casting.

Hooking a fish is only halfway to catching a fish. **Landing a fish** is what fishing is all about. However, to young anglers the actual catch is often not as important as the process of fishing. Don't take over and land your grandchild's fish. Missing a catch is part of fishing.

Explain and encourage **fishing ethics** to your grandchildren such as:

Follow the fishing regulations.
- Release undersized fish back to the water, unharmed, as soon as possible.
- Never take more fish than you need.
- Conserve the fishing environment – take your rubbish away with you.
- Do not allow your grandchildren to play with fish like toys.

Grandparent tips

- Waiting for a fish to bite can be frustrating for young anglers. If your grandchildren reach their top frustration level, pack up and go fishing another time.
- Keep fishing knives sheathed and out of young grandchildren's reach.
- Keep small fingers away from sharp hooks.
- Find out if there is any dangerous marine life in the area, for example, stonefish.
- Never take chances with the weather. Leave the boat at home if the weather looks at all dodgy.
- Handle fish with care. Make grandchildren aware that most fish have protective spines.

Tuna cakes

Young children will enjoy making and shaping these tuna cakes – especially if they have had a disappointing day out fishing and have arrived home without a catch.

Age level: 5–12 years

Number of children: any

What you need:
- A vegetable peeler.
- A medium-sized mixing bowl.
- A potato masher or fork.
- Measuring cups and spoons.
- A can opener.
- A knife.
- A cutting board.
- A plate.
- An oven tray.
- A non-stick frying pan.
- A colander.

Ingredients:
2 medium potatoes, peeled
1 tablespoon butter
425 g can tuna, drained and flaked
1 small onion, peeled and chopped
2 tablespoons chopped parsley
1 egg
pepper to taste
1 cup breadcrumbs
oil for frying if you don't use a non-stick frying pan
1 lemon, sliced

What to do:

- ◉ Cook the potatoes until tender. Drain well.
- ◉ Place the potatoes in a mixing bowl. Add butter and mash the potatoes.
- ◉ Combine the potatoes with the drained, flaked tuna.
- ◉ Add the chopped onion to the tuna mixture.
- ◉ Add parsley and egg, and season with pepper.
- ◉ Mix everything together well.
- ◉ Shape the mixture into round or fish shapes.
- ◉ Pour the breadcrumbs onto a plate. Gently coat each fish cake in crumbs.
- ◉ Put the fish cakes on an oven tray and place in the refrigerator for 1 hour, or for at least 15 minutes if your grandchildren are hungry.
- ◉ Heat the frying pan. Add oil if using a non-stick frying pan.
- ◉ Cook the fish cakes over a gentle heat until they are golden brown on both sides.
- ◉ To serve, garnish with lemon slices.

💡 Grandparent tip

- You can substitute tinned salmon for the tuna or an equal amount of cooked fish.

Sea, surf and sand

Most children love to spend time at the beach, playing on the sand and swimming or bodysurfing in the sea. Visit the beach early in the morning or late in the afternoon so you can avoid the sun at its strongest.

Age level: 3–12 years

Number of children: any

What you need:

- Be sun smart. Make sure you all use SPF15+ to SPF30+ sunscreen, wear sunhats, long-sleeved shirts and sunglasses.
- Beach umbrellas or shelters, and comfortable beach chairs make life easier at the beach.
- Take a supply of cool drinks and play equipment.

Grandparents need to be especially vigilant when caring for small grandchildren when they are near water. Keep in mind the following **safety considerations**:

- Swim only at beaches patrolled by lifesavers. Make sure your grandchildren swim between the red and yellow flags.
- Read safety signs. They are your guide to potential dangers and daily conditions at the beach.
- Ask a lifesaver for advice if you are unsure of surf conditions.
- Never allow your grandchildren to swim alone or at night.
- Never allow your grandchildren to run or dive into the water, even if you have checked the water. Water conditions can change rapidly.

Sand is an excellent surface for young grandchildren to draw on and practise their writing. **Sand sculpting** is the trendy term for building sandcastles. Taking along a few useful tools such as a bucket and spade will enable your grandchildren to create extraordinary creations from sand.

The beach is a wonderful place to discover the **tracks, trails and patterns** made by sea birds and sea creatures on the sand.

Beachcombing and rock pooling

Beachcombing is a relaxing activity you can share with your grandchildren. Combing the beach for washed-up treasures such as shells, seaweed and feathers is great fun. Different seasons bring different treasures, especially after storms.

Rock pools are fascinating places for grandchildren to explore. They are full of sea life such as seaweed, snails, crabs, sponges and other small sea creatures.

Age level: 3–12 years

Number of children: any

What you need:
- Suitable footwear, sunhat and a long-sleeved shirt.
- A jacket to keep out the wind.
- Sunscreen.

Seashore safety code
- Try not to touch sea animals and remember that rocks are homes for many sea animals. Replace rocks carefully.
- Do not put your hands where you cannot see them.
- Do not remove live sea animals from their environment.
- Return collected objects to where you found them.
- Watch out for waves.
- Read and take notice of signs.

Caution: Most rock pool creatures are harmless but a few can be dangerous to humans, such as the blue-ringed octopus.

Underwater viewer

An underwater viewer is a useful piece of equipment when you go rock pooling or ponding. The underwater viewer acts like a magnifying glass so your grandchildren will be able to watch life under the water – or in a rockpool.

Age level: 8–12 years

Number of children: any

What you need:
- A large, clean, empty can.
- A can opener.
- Waterproof sticky tape.
- Strong clear plastic wrap.

What to do:
- Remove the bottom of the can with a can opener so it is open at both ends.
- Make sure both ends of the can are smooth. Bind them with waterproof sticky tape.
- Cover one end of the can with clear plastic wrap.
- Bind the plastic wrap tightly to the tin with waterproof sticky tape.
- Push the sealed end of the can into the water. The water will press against the plastic and push it up, making the viewer act like a magnifying glass. Your grandchildren will now be able to see what's happening in the water.

Grandparent tip
- Another option for handy grandparents is to cut off the bottom of an old plastic bucket and cover one end with clear plastic wrap.

Sailing

Messing about in boats is a wonderful way for grandparents and grandchildren to spend time together.

If you have a hankering to sail, you can enrol in a sailing school with your grandchildren. Most sailing clubs run summer schools for beginners – young and old. If you are an experienced sailor, you will have completed navigation courses as well as resuscitation and first-aid courses.

Seasickness hints

- Take motion sickness tablets.
- Eat wisely. Dried biscuits are good.
- Don't watch others being sick.
- Stuff cotton wool up your nose: sickness is often related to smell.
- Look at the horizon, not the waves.
- Don't go below deck in bad weather.

Bottle boats

Your grandchildren can make a fleet of boats from bottles of different shapes, providing an exciting nautical experience for young grandchildren.

Age level: 5–8 years

Number of children: any

What you need:

- Plastic bottles with lids (all shapes and sizes).
- Strong glue.
- Extra lids.
- Strong cardboard.
- Scissors.
- Coloured paper.
- Wooden skewers.

What to do:

- Select a bottle. Make sure the lid is screwed on tightly.
- Glue on extra lids for funnels. Cut out cabins and crew from cardboard and glue them onto the boat. A sail can be made from paper and a wooden skewer.

Paddleboat

A paddleboat is a more complicated model for older grandchildren.

Age level: 8–12 years

Number of children: any

What you need:

- Two pieces of stiff card measuring 50 mm x 70 mm.
- Scissors.
- A rubber band.
- A piece of polystyrene cut into a boat shape measuring 25 mm x 175 mm x 350 mm.
- A container of water.

What to do:

- Cut slots in each piece of card (see Figure 1).
- Push one card inside the other to form a cross shape (see Figure 1).
- Place the rubber band around the stiff card (see Figure 2) and also around the end of the polystyrene boat shape (see Figure 3).
- Use your fingers to wind the stiff card (the paddle) until the rubber band is twisted tightly.
- Carefully place the paddleboat into the container of water. Release the paddle and watch the boat move in the water.

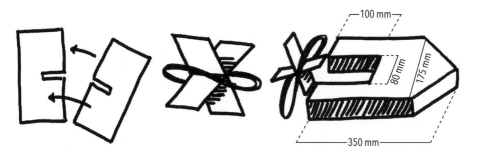

Figure 1   Figure 2   Figure 3

Travel games

Travel games are essential when travelling with grandchildren – either by air, car or train. Electronic games and devices to play DVDs and CDs are brilliant lifesavers when travelling with grandchildren.

Join the dots

The skill in this game lies in drawing lines that will prevent an opponent from completing too many boxes, but which help you complete lots of boxes when your turn comes.

Age level: 8–12 years

Number of children: 2 players

What you need:

✎ Paper and pencils.

How to play:

✪ Draw dots over a page in rows, both horizontally and vertically. A normal arrangement is 10 rows of dots.

✪ The first player joins two dots together. Diagonal lines are not allowed.

✪ The next player is allowed to join another two dots together.

✪ Once a player completes a box by joining two dots, they can write their initials in it.

✪ The winner is the player who completes the most boxes.

10 and you're out

Age level: 8–12 years

Number of children: 2 players

What you need:
- Paper and pencils.

How to play:
- One of the players thinks of a secret word and marks a dash for each of its letters on a piece of paper.
- The other player tries to guess which letters make up the word.
- If one of the letters they nominate is correct, the first player writes it on the dash where it belongs.
- If a wrong guess is made, the player has a point against them.
- The game continues until either the secret word is guessed or there are ten marks against the player.

Words from words

A fun word game to play with grandchildren.

Age level: 8–12 years

Number of children: 2 players

What you need:
- Paper and pencils.

How to play:
- Grandparents write a word on a piece of paper. It must have at least six letters.
- Each player must see how many words they can make from the original word.

I spy with my little eye

Age level: 5–12 years

Number of children: any

What you need:

✎ No equipment required but a sharp set of eyes is helpful!

'I spy' is an old favourite and one of the best travel games.

How to play:

⚙ A player chooses an object and says, 'I spy with my little eye something beginning with ...', inserting the initial of the object they've chosen.

⚙ The player who guesses the correct answer chooses the next object.

⚙ The game can be limited to objects found inside the car, train or plane or outside.

Alphabet shopping game

Age level: 5–12 years

Number of children: any

What you need:

- No equipment required but a good memory is helpful!

How to play:

- Each player must remember the list of items bought at the market and add another item. For example:
  Player 1: I went to the supermarket and I bought apples.
  Player 2: I went to the supermarket and I bought apples and bananas.
  Player 3: I went to the supermarket and I bought apples, bananas and cherries.
- If a player can't remember an item, gets the order of items wrong or can't think of a new item, they are out until the next round.

Variations:

- Aunt Agnes went to Adelaide and she took an Aardvark. The second item must have the initial B and so on. For example, Aunt Agnes went to Adelaide and she bought an Aardvark and a Bear.
- I went on holiday and I packed …
- At the beach I saw a …
- As I crept through the rainforest I saw a …

Number plate game

Age level: 8–12 years

Number of children: any

What you need:
- No equipment required but best played in a car!

How to play:
- Players can keep a list of number plates that make words.
- Players could also look for number plates that can be rearranged to make words.
- Players can make messages out of the letters. For example, WFD 567 could be 'What's for dinner?'

'Spotto' games

'Spotto' games work beautifully as travel games and there are many different versions.

Age level: 8–12 years

Number of children: any

What you need:
- No equipment required but best played in a car!

How to play:
- Players sit quietly and observe different things out of the window.
- For example, spot the yellow cars, brown cows, police stations, telephone boxes, clock towers or petrol stations.
- Players could also spot certain kinds of cars, with different cars scoring higher points (for example, ten points for a Ferrari).
- Players could look for number plates from interstate (one point).
- The first player to spot an object scores a point. The highest score wins.

Moving finger game

Age level: 5–12 years

Number of children: any

What you need:

📝 No equipment required.

How to play:

◎ Choose a well-known fairy story or make up an original story.

◎ The first player begins to tell the story, then stops and points to another player. This player must continue from where the story left off. They then point to another player to continue the story and so on.

◎ Alternatively, the first player has to tell a joke or riddle. They then point to another player to tell a joke or riddle.

◎ Make sure everyone has a chance to take a turn.

Snow trips

If you live close enough, a day trip to the snowfields can be exciting for grandchildren and will not stretch the budget or grandparents' nerves. Remember to pack extra clothing and plastic bags to take home wet clothing and footwear!

Snowflakes

Age level: 3–8 years

Number of children: any

What you need:
- Squares of white paper.
- Scissors.

You can make snowflakes for your grandchildren using squares of white paper.

What to do:
- Fold the square of paper on the diagonal.
- Fold again, and again.
- Cut off the top of the cone using a wavy or zigzag line.
- Make some cuts to the sides of the cone. Be careful not to cut all the way across.
- When your grandchildren unfold the paper, they will see their snowflake.
- Decorate the room with the snowflakes.

Grandparent tip
- Older grandchildren can make snowflakes using a circle of paper, folding it into twelfths, and making interesting cut-outs from the top and sides.

Part two:
How to thrive as a grandparent

Grandparenting 101

Grandparenting can be joyous, but it can also be tricky, challenging and frequently chaotic as we all manage increasingly complex lives. The image of grandparents sitting in rocking chairs on the veranda has vanished completely. Today's grandparents are busier than ever; but they can still play a vital role in their grandchildren's lives.

Luckily, you don't need special qualifications to become a grandparent. In fact, you can't even predict or choose *when* you will become a grandparent. It just happens. Sometimes quite suddenly – out of the blue, even. Grandparents with years of experience under their belt can find that they are revisiting their role when a new grandchild arrives for many reasons, including changes in the lives of their children such as a second marriage or a blended family.

Your role as a grandparent

Happily, **changes in modern family patterns** can also mean that you don't need blood ties to be a grandparent or a special person in a child's life. You don't even have to be 'old' – depending on the age of your partner, you can be an amazingly young grandparent.

Regardless, grandparents continue to play a special role in giving hugs and kisses to the young, listening and encouraging their grandchildren's sense of discovery and imagination.

Many grandparents are still working, some are caring for elderly parents and all have their own lives and commitments. Your age, health and where you live can also affect the role you are able to play within your new family.

Taking the time to think through **your role as a grandparent** and gently discussing your thoughts with your adult children – while understanding and acknowledging their expectations, too – can be an important conversation to have *before* a new grandchild is born.

One of the biggest misunderstanding in families when a new baby is born can be the mismatch between your children's expectations of how much **practical help** you, as grandparents, can give – and the reality of what you are willing, or able, to provide. Many grandparents enjoy their retirement and feel unable to commit to a heavy childcaring role if their adult children return to work and need or want their support.

Others find that caring for grandchildren is a pleasure that brings meaning to their lives, regardless of the amount of time and effort involved. Understand that your thoughts on the matter may also change once the baby has arrived, as your own circumstances or health changes or as the grandchildren grow into new and exciting stages.

Be mindful also that many independent, sometimes older, children can find the sudden involvement and expectations of their parents, or parents-in-law, takes some adjusting to. **New roles are being defined and old ones updated.** It takes time to find a new equilibrium amid such excitement and investment all round as relationships are challenged, deepened and hopefully strengthened.

This is where **grandparent classes**, run through the maternity wing of a hospital, can be a great way to understand the current trends and challenges of caring for a baby. Parenting in general, such as the changing role of fathers and how best to support new parents, is also often covered. The classes are there to enhance your relationship with your children and their partners, and alleviate some of the misunderstandings and tensions that can arrive with the new roles, expectations and enthusiasm that a new baby can bring. These usually short, one-off sessions can also cover birth choices, swaddling, new feeding and sleeping information, as well as the correct use of car seats. There are many online or telephone helplines you can also contact to talk through any issues you may be having. Contact your local council, library or community centre for assistance.

As a grandparent, **taking care to provide help and advice** when it is wanted or asked for, and standing back when it isn't, can do much for your relationship with the parents of your grandchild. Don't be offended if your family is gaining knowledge from health professionals, books or helplines. There is a wonderful support system out there for parents and a wide range of expert opinions that can also be daunting at times for the first-time parent.

Instead, listening to your children (and their partners) and their concerns and joys at this time – as well as being a sounding board and supporting them in their decisions – will give them confidence in their parenting and foster their own sense of intuition as to what is right for *their* baby. It will also deepen their trust of you, doing wonders for your relationship with them, and by extension, your grandchildren.

Family relationships can become more complicated when a grandchild arrives. You know your own child best, their personality and their needs and wants at this time, so be guided by this knowledge foremost. Consider the following.

- Be mindful of what your family actually finds helpful by gently asking and being open to what you can do to help – it may not be what you think, or what you would have expected. One friend's daughter-in-law politely suggested that it would be more helpful to her if the grandmother could mind the grand-daughter while she worked from home. In this way, she could earn money to afford a cleaner rather than have her mother-in-law clean the house. She retained her independence and continued working – and it gave her mother-in-law time with the grand-daughter rather than the dishes!
- Unconditional support of birth decisions and breastfeeding decisions, for example, will make everyone feel more comfortable. Be especially sensitive if it has been a difficult or traumatic birth and understand that there may be teary patches, especially a few days after the birth. Be sensitive to what the mother and parents need at this sometimes overwhelming and physically and emotionally exhausting time.
- Discuss ahead of time what expectations the parents, and the mother in particular, have about visiting the newborn both at the hospital and at home. Everyone is different and some are more comfortable than others

with visitors at this time. Be respectful of the short time the new father may also have off work, remembering what a special bonding time this is for a new family.

- Calling or messaging ahead to arrange or confirm a visit to the newborn grandchild can be helpful as sudden arrivals can be disruptive. If you live at a distance, arranging an online Skype connection for a convenient time might also be appreciated.

- If you will be looking after older grandchildren around the birth of the new grandchild, have practice sleepovers in your or the family's home ahead of time so that you are familiar with the children's routine and care.

- Once the new family is home, offers to bring meals or stock the freezer can be really appreciated. Offering to help with the housework (washing or putting away dishes, doing or folding washing or sweeping floors) or looking after the baby (or older children) may be helpful (however, see above). Time at your house for a meal or a play for the older children may also be welcome.

Becoming a grandparent is different for everyone. Some grandparents have been waiting for years and know exactly what they want to be called – Grandma, Grandpa, Nana, Pop, Ma, Gramps, Gran, Oma, Opa, Nonna, Nonno. Some youthful grandparents are dismayed at the prospect and wonder, 'Can't I just be called Harry?' Be prepared that, whatever you decide, when your grandchild is learning to talk you may end up with a completely different, but still loving, name anyway!

If you are part of a blended family, and one of a number of grandparents, be sensitive and diplomatic when choosing or discussing **what you want to be called** – your first choice may already be taken. If you do find yourself as the third, fourth (or maybe more) set of grandparents, tread lightly and take time to find your position in the new family structure. If you can't see a role for yourself when the new grandchild is born, don't worry, you will have many opportunities to bond with your grandchild as they grow – and remember, school holiday care is always in demand!

Finally, in the excitement of becoming a grandparent again or for the first-time, try and **avoid burnout from over-committing yourself**. Remember, other grandchildren may follow and it can cause issues in a family if one adult child has more access to your childcare services than other siblings have or had. Young children can also be exhausting, and looking after yourself, including keeping your own interests, means you ultimately have more energy for the little ones.

Finally, a note on **grandparenting from a distance** as not all grandparents are able to live close to their families. One grandchild I know is convinced that his much-loved grandparents live at the airport! But living away doesn't necessarily mean a diminished relationship with your children or grandchildren, or that you are unable to help in other ways.

Emails, text messages, Facebook, Skype and sharing blogs can all mean you and your grandchildren can share time, conversations and images, bringing the relationship to life at a very small cost. You can also play chess and other games online together, using modern technology to connect in ways previously unknown. If you are missing a hands-on grandparenting role there are many single parents with young children who will welcome a stand-in grandparent.

While it can be lovely to send an email on holidays or Skype from time to time, don't feel pressured to use this form of communication if it is not your thing. Thankfully, young children still get a thrill out of something arriving in the mail. Checking the mail is a lovely responsibility for a little one, and watching out for the postman – an exciting event in a little one's day – can be made even more special when there is the possibility that someone they love has sent them something.

Sending old-fashioned cards, postcards, letters and small parcels by **snail mail** is a lovely way to connect and communicate with grandchildren. A friend's grandson loves collecting postcards sent from her travels and has put them in a special box. For our grandchildren, communicating this way may end up as a museum exhibit in the future!

Naturally, birthday and Christmas presents coming through the mail can be very exciting for little ones, too. Mark on the calendar special events coming up in your grandchildren's lives such as speech nights, school performances, birthdays, sports finals etc. so you can communicate at these special times.

How your grandchild will develop

The main thing to remember is that every child is different. Some children acquire physical, intellectual and social skills earlier than others. All children develop at their own rate and there is a wide range of 'average'.

Newborn babies

It is such a special miraculous event when your newborn grandchild arrives. Enjoy watching and observing your grandchild develop into a unique human being. Keep up to date with the changes in caring for babies – they have been huge since our children were born. Keep your counsel and enjoy the cuddles.

Older babies (3–12 months)

This is a stage of tremendous change. Remember some babies will reach some stages sooner, some later. As you watch your grandchild's development you will see them change from a helpless baby into a small person with their own personality. At this stage grandchildren can crawl or pull and reach up to furniture, stand or walk. You will be observing your grandchild's first steps, sounds and words. Remember: nearly everything goes into your grandchild's mouth at this stage.

Toddlers (12 months–3 years)

Life for a toddler is one big adventure. They will be exploring and seeing how things work. They will master new skills and begin to talk to you. During this time of great change your grandchild will advance to building constructions and completing a jigsaw puzzle. Their artistic efforts will progress from scribbles to labelled pictures and imaginative craft constructions. They will love to copy what you are doing such as helping around the house. Playing with water, such as helping with the washing up or blowing bubbles, is popular. They will enjoy opportunities for make-believe play with basic props such as boxes, curtains, blankets, and of course a box of dress-ups. Creative play with cutting and pasting is always fun and there should always be lots of time to explore outdoors.

Pre-schooler (3–5 years)

During the pre-school years, your grandchildren begin to learn the important skills of socialisation and independence. They have now acquired coordination and continue social and language development. There will be many new surroundings and experiences. They may be attending preschool sessions within their formal childcare setting or attending sessions at their local preschool or school. They will be climbing with agility, kicking, catching, throwing balls, riding bicycles and enjoying games at this stage. They will be enjoying learning through informal play.

Young school child (5–8 years)

At about five or six years, your grandchildren will begin their formal education at school. Grandchildren's social and learning skills make leaps and bounds once they are at school. During their early school years, your grandchild will become a reader and writer and capable of simple arithmetic. They will delight in the world around them and you will be able to share discoveries with them. Playing board games, making things, exploring the outdoors and spending special days with your grandchildren will provide lasting memories.

The older school child (8–12 years)

At this stage, your grandchild is well on the road to independence. You can take your grandchild on outings and show them skills you have gained that will stay with them forever. This is a time for talking about, and more importantly listening, to what your grandchildren are finding out about life. It is also a time when grandchildren may be able to help you keep up with the latest developments in technology. You will be able to become someone they can trust and rely on – someone who can provide a safe haven from their complex and busy lives, if they ever need one.

Be prepared

Whether you live nearby or further away, your home can be a wonderful place for the grandchildren to visit and provide a welcome home-away-from-home for tired parents. Making a few preparatations ahead of time can make the visit smoother and more enjoyable for everyone. Don't forget to ask if there is anything specific that the new parents would find useful.

If you have the space or you are going to babysit on a regular basis, **equipment** such as cots (portable cots are good as they can be packed away), baby chairs, car seats and prams stored at your home can save time and effort for everyone. Don't be daunted by long lists of baby equipment that is supposedly needed when a grandchild comes to visit or feel you need to purchase everything. Reputable baby equipment hire firms can also meet most baby needs for short- or long-term visits.

Charity shops and garage sales as well as online sellers on eBay and Gumtree are excellent places to buy **pre-loved equipment** (although it is generally not recommended that you buy mattresses or car seats in this way). If you are buying baby equipment, make sure it meets national safety standards – many old cots have unsafe designs and can cause accidents. Be careful with bunk beds also. Car seats for young children must also meet safety standards.

A **pram, pusher or stroller** is important equipment for grandparents when caring for their grandchildren. The 'nanny' style of pram is still available for gentle strolls in the park, but the modern pram has undergone many changes. Prams today have to meet stringent safety regulations, work efficiently on a variety of surfaces and fold to be taken on public transport or carried in the boot of the family car – as well as have somewhere to fit the shopping! Some prams even have a space on the end for an older toddler to sit or a board for them to stand on.

Buying a pram

A grandparent's offer to buy a pram for the new grandchild can sometimes break the budget. Beware of pram showroom sales people, too. When they see a grandparent as a customer, their sales attack can be enthusiastic to say the least.

The type of pram your family prefers will depend on their lifestyle, so consult them first and do some research online before racing off to buy a top-of-the-range item. Look for a well-made pram which will give you value for money and light and practical construction – it is a lot heavier when you are lifting it into a boot! Handles that can be adjusted for different heights can be helpful, too.

Remember, discount department stores also have cheap strollers that can be easily stored and used for extra or occasional use at your home or theirs.

Pram safety

There are some issues around **pram safety** that are worth being aware of.

- Never leave a baby unattended in a pram.
- Check your grandchild is fastened safely and comfortably into the pram – always. A young grandchild can easily and quickly slide down the pram with the movement as you stride along. Even small children that can sit up still need to be strapped in.
- Don't overload the handles with shopping – it is very easy for the pram to tip over.
- Practise collapsing the pram until you can do it quickly and efficiently before setting off with your grandchild.
- Always use the brakes when you stop and double check they are on firmly at roads, train platforms and on slopes.

Planning ahead for when your grandchildren visit can be helpful. Have a selection of **simple activities** prepared that you can share with your grandchildren so you can spend relaxed and happy times together. Children often enjoy the time spent with you chatting as well as being involved in simple activities like baking a cake, going for a walk or to the park, a ride on the train, a trip to the local library, fire station or café.

Having a **basic collection of toys** on-hand for grandchildren to play with at your home is also a good idea. Again, they don't need to be an expensive or expansive collection. Garage sales, school fetes or discount shops like Ikea and Aldi are fabulous. Charity shops and book fairs can be good places to pick up a few things, too. Online sites such as eBay or Gumtree are also helpful too as they can post to you. (Remember to be careful that toys are safe with no small parts that can be removed or swallowed such as buttons for eyes on soft toys.)

Tips on sharing

Expecting a grandchild to share his favourite teddy with another grandchild can cause untold problems! Very young children especially are not capable of understanding the idea of sharing. Keeping lots of soft cuddly toys in residence at your house that children can feel are their own – and don't need to be shared with other visitors – can go a long way to avoiding disputes, and can make your place feel like a home away from home with familiar and predictable items. Having plenty of other equipment such as blocks, puzzles, paint, brushes, pens and paper on hand can minimise problems, too (see below).

Some parents may also welcome you storing any overflow of toys they have as they can easily get out of hand at home, especially after birthdays! A friend managed to find some of her own children's toys and books she had stashed away and the grandchildren love playing with Mum and Dad's original **retro items**!

Depending on your grandchildren's interests, now may also be a good time to dust off the tools or the sewing machine and **make a few toys or outfits**, too.

Following are some basic ideas to keep the little ones occupied.

- Books of all kinds – board books, picture books, activity books as well as non-fiction titles on different topics like space, animals, castles etc. depending on your and the children's interests.
- Blocks of all shapes, sizes and colours. Lego is always popular as kids get older.
- Containers suitable for water or sand play – although the tupperware drawer remains a perennial favourite.
- Cars, trucks, planes and ships, plastic fences and road mats, if possible.
- Sets of zoo or farm animals.
- Dolls, prams, tea-sets and kitchen play utensils – again, your own drawers can be very enticing to little ones.
- Cash register and a collection of empty containers for playing shop.
- Carpentry sets and doctor sets to promote role-playing.

- Old clothes for dress-ups.
- Boxes and recycling materials for construction.

Sandpits make excellent play areas for young grandchildren and best of all, you don't need a large area or to redesign your garden. Try the following ideas.

- Use an empty paddling pool (these often look like plastic shells) to hold the sand. You can also use an old tyre which can be bought from a wrecker or garage. (The top will need to be sliced off.)
- Fill the sandpit with sand. (This can be purchased from hardware stores or building suppliers).
- Stock the sandpit with plastic containers of all shapes and sizes, buckets and spades.
- Cover the sandpit at night to keep animals out and to keep it dry. An upturned bucket under the cover will stop a puddle from gathering on the cover when it is raining.

A simple hose in hot weather or a sprinkler depending on any water restrictions can be heaps of fun, as can paddling pools. Remember grandchildren will need constant supervision while they are **playing with water.**

Set up the pool on the grass rather than on cement or concrete – it will be less slippery underfoot. Old plastic containers will provide hours of fun. Putting a basin of water beside the pool so children can step into it before getting into the pool will keep the pool free of grass and dirt. Empty or cover the pool after use.

Keep a few bath toys or more plastic containers in the bathroom so children can play while getting clean. Bubblebath is also fun. Children also love playing in the kitchen sink, so keep a footstool or chair handy and make sure there are no sharp objects in the sink, just lots of bubbles!

Plan ahead

If you are caring for your grandchildren short or long-term, planning your day(s) or week(s) efficiently can give you a headstart. Of course, allow for your own personality and tolerance for chaos or order and desire for spontaneity.

Making a list of activities, ideas or meals ahead of time for the time the grandchildren will be with you can be very helpful. As can **preparing activities** ahead of time by:

- making play dough
- organising materials for a collage or painting
- hunting out suitable gardening tools or fishing gear
- checking out times of TV programs to watch, CDs and DVDs to borrow, cinema times or events.

Also consider how you will get around with the children. For example, if you can walk to the park or will need to drive? What will you do if the weather is bad and you can't escape outside the house? Above all, be flexible. It's every grandparent's right to abandon plans and live in the moment!

School holidays are when grandparents are absolutely indispensable, coming into their own as fill-the-gap specialists. Whether you are minding the grandchildren for a day or a week, a little forward planning can make the most of this precious time, too.

There are always lots of **activities** planned for the school holidays. Watch, read and check the local media for information on available activities. You can always visit local facilities such as the library, park or swimming pool ahead of time to find out the opening times and if special activities are provided during holidays. Try looking up museums or galleries in the city, too. Take note of dates, opening times, place and age-level suitability of facilities or activities. Be aware that some activities need to be booked and paid for in advance – don't forget to book early to avoid missing out!

Grandchildren also appreciate a little **down time** in the school holidays too, so don't forget to balance activities with days at home doing quiet things like drawing, watching movies, reading and playing games. In the rush of the school term, it can be hard to find time to play snakes and ladders or teach a child how to play chess, but in the school holidays, and with a grandparent, these things can be very special.

Try including children in your usual **favourite activities**, such as gardening. Enlist the children to help. Grandchildren can rake leaves, fill wheelbarrows and spend hours watching worms! Small children especially can find an adventure in the mundane – and it also teaches them that you don't need to be doing something amazing or expensive to have a good time. These are the times that children will often open up and you can talk about their worries with them. There can also be the times to talk about your childhood memories, show them old family photographs and memorabilia such as a family member's war medals.

Long-term care

Many grandparents take on long-term care of their grandchildren for many reasons – parents' work commitments, the arrival of a new baby or ill health of a parent, school holiday care etc. Some planning and forward thinking in this situation can be particularly beneficial and can help make the time you spend with your grandchildren both rewarding and fun. Following are some ideas.

- Keep a temporary calendar large enough to note the grandchildren's activities. Older grandchildren can be responsible for writing their own activities on the calendar.
- Use support systems and services around you. Government child health centres are a good place to start.
- Find local playgroups (often held at community centres or local churches) and storytime at local libraries. The can often be a good way of meeting other people and swapping ideas or local information for kids, as well as fun-filled playtime for kids with others their own age.
- Involve the other grandparents – they may be happy to help, and you may enjoy the time to catch up with another adult.

- Plan menus and shopping. Think about food that can easily be taken with you when you are out. Have some containers, drink bottles or ice bricks on hand. Make a meal that everyone can enjoy. Plan and freeze food ahead. Every time you cook or bake, double, treble or quadruple the quantities and add the date of freezing on the packaging.
- Make sure you and the grandchildren escape from the the house every day, even just for a short walk. The fresh air will do everyone good and the exercise can help little ones rest better later.
- Remember, don't worry too much about trying to keep a tidy house. Work as a team to pack up one activity before starting another. Make a game of cleaning up. Play music to pack up to in a set time.

Finally, watch your **energy levels** and avoid becoming irritable and exhausted by over-committing yourself with babysitting or childcare. Watch you don't bottle up stress, too, this could lead to an explosion that could be harmful and frightening for grandchildren.

Most importantly, **find time for yourself**, partners and friends. Take a few minutes to phone, text, email, Twitter or Facebook a friend or the family. Communicating with an adult will give you a lift. If you're looking after grandchildren on a long-term live-in basis, arrange with a friend or neighbour to babysit occasionally so you can go out, take a rest or keep up with friends or activities for yourself. Don't be afraid to say 'no' occasionally, too.

Visiting

Some families make a **regular visit** to the grandparents every week, perhaps a weeknight to share the load or a weekend lunch. For some, perhaps it's just the occasional visit. Either way, a little planning can prevent these visits turning into horror outings for everyone. Following are some suggestions to make the visit a pleasant time together – a welcome event, which gives grandchildren an opportunity to play and adults time to talk. As grandchildren get older, they will enjoy joining in on these discussions too, or helping prepare a meal.

- Don't make a fuss. Explain that you're quite happy for everyone to leave whenever they feel like it or need to. Sometimes young children can run out of puff quite quickly and a sudden departure is necessary.

- Provide a simple meal. Something everyone will eat and enjoy or maybe you can order from your favourite takeaway outlet?
- If your grandchildren are quite young and eat early, provide a simple meal for them before the adults' dinner. Young grandchildren can then be bathed and in pyjamas, perhaps while the adults' dinner is in the oven. This can make for a smooth transition to bedtime when everyone goes home.
- It may help busy working parents if you arrange to pick up grandchildren from school on the night of the family visit, helping with homework if possible.

A visiting grandparent's survival kit

If you occasionally have sleepovers at your grandchildren's home or are likely to be called out on an emergency visit, it can be a good idea to have a **survival kit** ready to pick up and go.

- laptop, tablet, smart phone or other devices plus cords and chargers
- gaming console if you want to play games and/or continue your exercise regime
- portable radio
- torch
- travel alarm clock
- medication and copies of prescriptions
- easy-to-wash clothes and comfortable shoes
- books or magazines or an e-reader with chargers
- a reading light and battery
- a nightlight for your room or halls or corridors nearby.

Staying over

Alternatively, if your family occasionally stays over due to time, distance, convenience or just for the fun of it, how do you squeeze a family of three, four or more (parents and grandchildren) into your home which usually accommodates one or two adults and a pet or two? Moreover, what if they are moving in for a period of time either between houses, or while renovations are being carried out?

It may help to imagine that your home's floor plan is flexible. The office can be moved into your bedroom; the dining and sitting rooms can become bedrooms. Take care to keep your own private space, though, even if your bedroom is crowded with office, art and craft, fishing or golf equipment! Following are a few more ideas.

- If the weather is reasonable, can you hire a caravan or tent?
- Can you buy extra mattresses or borrow them and other equipment from friends to save buying these things?
- Consider if surplus furniture can be stored in the shed or garage when not needed.
- Ask for help to move any heavy furniture.
- Allocate a sleeping area and place for each grandchild's bag and belongings. These areas can be the responsibility of the grandchild.
- Arrange for separate sleeping spaces for older and younger grandchildren. Older grandchildren usually like to stay up late to chat, read in bed or play their computer games. Younger grandchildren should go to bed early!
- If necessary, and they are already used to sleeping in a bed, small children can 'top-and-tail' – place a pillow at each end of the bed and one large or two small blankets or doonas/duvets over the top of them.
- Sharing a room can be very exciting, especially for kids who don't usually share a room, so be prepared for some giggling and allow some extra time for kids to settle.
- There are some very good blow-up mattresses that come in a variety of sizes, and discount department stores or camping stores have sleeping bags, which can be fun for children, too.
- If you need to update your lounge, consider replacing it with something that can either turn into a bed or has some storage capabilities.
- Do you have room for a daybed somewhere? These can easily transform from a lounge to a bed, taking up little extra space.
- Set up a few rules to maintain order and consideration for both guests and hosts (see below).

- Allocate a quiet space in your home – everyone needs some quiet space where they can reflect, play quietly, resolve problems, gather resources or just daydream!
- Safety-proof your home environment (see pages 294–299).

Finally, be mindful that when you return home from being with the family or when the grandchildren leave after being with you, there will be a period of readjustment. They may be sad to leave, or be looking forward to going home – and it may seem very quiet all of a sudden! It is good to know this and to be prepared for it.

Sleeping

Some young grandchildren can be better behaved for you than they are for their own parents. Even so, whether they are staying with you or you are looking after them in their own home, getting them to bed – much less getting them to actually **sleep** – can be tricky.

If you're able to keep to the family routine, with a bit of luck, young grandchildren will still take their **daytime nap** for you when you are caring for them. Make sure naps are early in the day so children are still sleepy around bedtime. A play at the park afterwards or an afternoon walk can make the transition to bedtime smoother. It can also help their appetite for dinner, too.

Give grandchildren plenty of warning before **bedtime**. For instance, tell them, 'Only ten more minutes to play before bedtime! Or, 'As soon as this TV program finishes it is bedtime!' Stick to your time limits and discourage starting a new game or watching a new TV program just before bedtime.

When you're putting your grandchildren to bed, turn your phone off or use your message machine as interruptions can set you back to square one. Say, 'Good night,' and leave the room quietly and quickly. If your grandchild comes out of the bedroom, take them back gently and firmly, but immediately.

Tips for bedtime

- If children have outgrown a nap, try setting aside a **rest or quiet time** instead at a regular time. Children can look through books, or do a puzzle, draw or listen to a story – while you have a rest, too.
- Try and keep to your grandchildren's **normal routine** for naps and bedtime as much as possible. Usually this is dinner, a short playtime, bath and a bedtime story, but check with the parents for what they usually do.
- A bedside lamp or **night light and favourite cuddly toy** can help your grandchild settle for sleep. They are also helpful when checking on a grandchild in the middle of the night.
- Playing **soothing music** at a low level can encourage a reluctant sleeper. Some children like to go to sleep to stories on CD, too (these can often be borrowed from your local library or found in op shops).
- Don't read or tell bedtime stories that are scary or boisterous.
- To stop grandchildren from falling out of bed, place the bed against the wall. Put cushions or some other 'landing pad' on the floor next to the bed to soften a **possible fall**.
- Tuck the top sheet lengthwise so there is a **good tuck-in** on each side to hold the grandchild firmly in bed or let them sleep on a mattress on the floor. (Watch your back!)
- If grandchildren keep getting out of bed for a **drink**, leave a drink bottle beside the bed. Be mindful, however, that young children may need to be taken to the toilet before you go to bed to stop children wetting the bed in the middle of the night or early in the morning.
- If your grandchildren are **early wakers** – and old enough to understand time – put a watch or clock in their room and explain what time it needs to be before they get up. If this doesn't work, again depending on their age, you can encourage them to amuse themselves quietly in the morning while you try to get a little more sleep. If this is the case, try leaving safe toys and books where they can reach them.

What's for dinner?

Thinking of meals and food to serve grandchildren and their families can be stressful. Check with parents about what grandchildren will – or might – eat! Be very careful if a grandchild has allergies to particular foods and always check with the parent if you are unsure of what to give them. Also, some grandchildren have very strong, or peculiar, likes and dislikes – and these can change from day to day.

Remember, there is no way you can change a grandchild's eating pattern or behaviour during the time they spend with you. The aim is to keep your grandchildren and their families happy, and at the same time, serve healthy meals.

Don't discard favourite family recipes for main meals or treats such as dessert or cakes and slices – many kids will be more inclined to try what you have made for them. Most can be used as is or modified slightly to make them a little plainer and more palatable. Many children are now used to a wide variety of tastes and cuisines, but the easiest, simplest dishes tend to still be the most popular. Reducing salt and spices in main dishes and the amount of sugar in cakes and biscuits can be quite easy, too. Be careful with colours and sugar and salt levels in pre-packaged food. Overdoing the colour or the sugar can have disastrous effects on some children, and can be cumulative.

- It's not difficult to provide healthy food for older grandchildren. Check with your family as to what children do and do not like!

The following are easy to prepare from things you probably already have in the cupboard or fridge.

- Breakfast: cereal and milk, fruit and toast.
- Mid-morning snack: fruit or plain biscuits and cheese, a sandwich.
- Lunch: soup and bread, fruit, drink of milk or yoghurt, or a sandwich filled with cheese, spreads or salad.
- Afternoon or after-school snack: fruit, yoghurt, milk drink, toast or plain biscuits.
- Dinner: grilled meats, vegies, rice, tins of tuna, avocado or pasta.

Tips for feeding babies and toddlers

- Do protect yourself and the eating area – use bibs, aprons and plastic sheeting for the table and floor. If you have a precious table with a beautiful surface, protect that, too.
- Set the table with cutlery that young grandchildren can handle easily.
- Use small cups with big handles or lids, unbreakable plates and bowls and washable tablecloths or mats.
- Have wipes handy.
- Don't have the television on or leave toys around to distract your grandchild when eating.
- Don't make mealtimes a battleground.

Technology

In a grandparent's lifetime, some modern gadgets now familiar were once science fiction. Computers of all sizes and shapes as well as tablets, smartphones and other devices play a vital part in our lives – and are being updated constantly and multiplying in number and range.

Families differ in their attitudes to children using and being exposed to technology. Some families think it's best to shield their young children from technology such as computer games. They prefer them to find other ways to beat boredom such as playing traditional games and activities where they interact with other people and the outdoors, or books or craft. These parents are happy for their children to be exposed to technology when they go to school. Other parents encourage their children to use a variety of technology in their own homes, use social networking sites and take part in a digital-heavy lifestyle. Above all, though, grandparents need to support the decisions their families have made.

Grandparent tip

- If you are a grandparent who is happy and content with your IT minimalist life, rest assured that virtual experiences derived from technology will never replace your grandchildren's own learning and entertainment through play, 'hands on' experiences, and time shared with you.

For many grandparents, tablets, computers and smartphones are highly valued, often providing life-saving links to their community. Explain to your grandchildren how important technology is in your life and ask them to respect your IT equipment as well as the boundaries and limits you set for their use when in your home.

If, however, you don't have your own computer, most libraries and community centres have computers available for public access and training facilities. There are also coffee shops and other commercial outlets and businesses such as email kiosks where you can use the internet and wi-fi services.

If you are not especially tech-savvy, your eager grandchildren will only be too happy to help you master computers and other devices. You can play games, share photos and build albums, communicate through writing, drawing, texting, e-cards and sharing music. You will be forever learning, discovering and exploring new ways with grandchildren to introduce technology into your life.

 Tip

- Work as a team and record grandchildren's instructions when they are showing you how a computer, device or gadget operates. This is good training for grandchildren and the recording of instructions will be a useful backup for you.

The internet, app stores, YouTube and social media are useful tools and resources for entertainment, information and communication. You can use the **internet** to locate information and help your grandchildren pursue interests and passions. You can help them master search strategies by helping them to find appropriate search words and terms to locate or verify a fact or information and assisting them to spell correctly. You can also assist in selecting appropriate sites or topics from the menu on never-ending topics such as dinosaurs, canoeing, collage making, how-to play a musical instrument, caring for caterpillars, where to go and how-to do stuff.

Apps are self-contained packets of information and entertainment to use on devices. You can purchase them at the click of a finger to use on your smartphone and devices such as tablets. (Another click of a finger and you can delete an app.) You can import apps that are often free such as a calculator or a torch, a weather forecasting service, football fixtures, games, e-books and other creative and learning applications appropriate to grandchildren's ages.

Tip

- A balance between books and e-book as well as traditional learning and entertainment is a good mix for grandchildren.

Many grandparents use **social media** such as Facebook, Twitter and blogging to communicate with family and friends. Never allow grandchildren to access your accounts or provide online content without your permission. Check with your grandchild's parents for appropriate cyber-safety practices when your grandchildren are using devices.

The internet has no regulatory body, no centralised content-control mechanisms and no advisory parental (or grandparental) warnings. Make sure your grandchildren are in friendly zones when they're using the internet – free of violence, pornography and other adult material. Schools often have safe sites or portals for children to use and can be a good safe way for children to browse the internet. Government websites also have important information and guidelines, often presented in an easy-to-understand way, if you are unsure of anything.

If your grandchildren are going to be using your computer frequently, install locked gateways with a filtering and monitoring software product or alter your system preferences to fit your family's requirements for their children's online use.

Tip

- Never underestimate a grandchild's ability to crack your computer password.

Instead of the board and outdoor games grandparents played as children, grandchildren are now using new gadgets for entertainment and interaction between their friends. Many grandchildren will be **video gaming** at some time on TV-connected consoles or hand-held devices such as Nintendo DS, iPod Touch, a PlayStation or Xbox. Young grandchildren could also be accessing games on computers, smartphones and tablets.

Many games present grandchildren with creative and problem-solving opportunities – a chance to cooperate and interact socially. Why not join in the fun? Hone your coordination skills and play with your grandchildren. Many IT-savvy grandparents may have already honed their video-gaming skills, but if you're not a video-gaming expert yet, request some tuition from grandchildren.

Video gaming guidelines

- Make sure your grandchildren are playing video games that are age-appropriate. Games have a classification and are rated like movies. (M and MA15 games are not for young grandchildren and can include explicit violence and obscene language.)
- Discuss weekly or daily screen time limits with your family.
- Control the amount of screen time the grandchildren are spending playing games in your care. You can set parameters when grandchildren are in your home and stick to them.
- Check with parents and research before you buy video games for your grandchildren. Go online for information and trial free samples.

A little planning will make life easier when grandchildren are using computer and other devices in your home.

■ Allocate a space in your home where grandchildren can use their computers and devices under your supervision – the kitchen bench is often a good place.

- If grandchildren are using *your* computer, make sure it is where you can keep an eye on its use and the screen. Agree on an appropriate allowance for screen time. (Don't forget to check with parents first!)
- Small screens do not work well when more than two grandchildren are using them for viewing or playing games. Set up a fair pattern of use if more than one grandchild is using your computer or playing games on your equipment.
- Set up a separate 'guest' access on your computer for grandchildren and use parental controls in 'preferences' for child-friendly access to games.
- Make sure your important data is backed up or safely locked away. It's amazing how young grandchildren – especially grandchildren with very tiny fingers – can find their way through your tablets and smartphones. Remember to lock your smartphone down before you hand it over to a bored grandchild for entertainment.

Some ideas for managing computer and other devices in your home

- Set up rules and filters to ensure emails from grandchildren and families are filed into specific mailboxes separate to your personal, business and junk emails, then star, flag, or colour-code the important emails to sort them.
- Organise your digital photos. Download them from your camera or phone regularly. Label them with your grandchildren's names, the date and place it was taken if you like and then sort them into folders.
- Have a ready-to-go library of appropriate games and e-books (many are free) available on screen to entertain grandchildren during down time when you're desperate for a cup of tea and a small portion of piece and quiet.
- Label your smartphones, tablets, computers, chargers and connecting cords with permanent markers so there is no confusion when big and small techies visit with their devices.

- Caution: Pet rabbits and dogs are very partial to nibbling on charger cords and connections.
- Finally, it's important that you, and your grandchildren, sit upright and don't stay in the same position too long when using a computer or other gadgets and devices. All IT users need to take breaks from the screen and keyboard.

Modern grandparents are aware that when grandchildren watch suitable **children's television programmes**, grandparents can gain some well-earned time out. Plan viewing times to suit your timetable, for example, late in the afternoon when you're desperate for a sit-down and a quiet cup of tea. Dedicated children's TV stations are only a click away when you are caring for grandchildren in your home, and there is a huge range of suitable DVDs.

Play an active role in your grandchildren's viewing. Read TV **viewing guides and reviews** of DVDs – they can often be found in the newspaper and specific magazines for parents. Discuss with your grandchildren the programmes they may watch when in your care and plan together what they will watch.

Choose programmes that are made for your grandchildren's age group. Check the suitability of programmes with your grandchildren's parents as well. You will observe that grandchildren are discerning and will gravitate to **programmes that are appropriate for their age** – although this can get tricky when you have a wide age range of children to cater to. While small children often like the older programming, make sure they also get their time with age-appropriate material so they don't miss out. Programmes that encourage singing and movement can be fun – don't forget to join in, too.

Caution: Don't let your grandchildren recognise your home as a place for non-stop TV viewing. Show no fear: turn off the TV!

 Tip

- Learn the **classification symbols** that indicate the level of suitability of a programme. (Classification symbols are also useful for watching videos, games, DVDs and films.)

The aim of **advertising** on TVs, tablets, and similar technology is to entice you, your grandchildren and their families to buy products. These advertisements are often unsuitable for young grandchildren. Use your remote control to turn off or mute ads.

✋ Tip

- Don't underestimate the information grandchildren are absorbing from TV. Talk with them about what they are watching, especially advertising, but also regular programming. Be active in expressing your values and encourage them to watch with a questioning attitude.

Supervise your grandchildren's viewing at all times. Be ready to turn off the TV as soon as something scary, violent or that doesn't meet your values comes on the screen. Get your grandchildren into the habit of turning off the TV as soon as a chosen program has finished.

Few families will disagree with having **child-friendly DVDs** at your home for grandchildren to view. Build up a collection or borrow suitable videos and DVDs from the library or video shop for when your grandchildren visit. Select videos or DVDs of movies or books you enjoyed when you were young. Introduce the accompanying books to your grandchildren.

Don't worry about very young grandchildren viewing the same program many times. Just as they enjoy the same storybook being read again and again, children love the repetition of a suitable video or DVD.

Tips for portable DVD players

- Portable DVD players can be a boon for grandparents. If your grandchildren have a portable DVD player at their home, encourage them to bring it with them when they visit you.
- They are also excellent long-distant travelling tools in the car or on a plane. A child-friendly DVD can last for many miles. You can stop the DVD, break your journey with a food and drink rest and make time for a 'run around'. Back in the car you can play another DVD until you get to the end of the journey.

- If you plan to use a portable DVD on a plane, battery life is critical. Battery life needs to last as long as the longest movie you or your grandchildren want to watch.
- Take a portable DVD player and a selection of DVDs if you need to escape and watch a not-suitable-for-children DVD when you're staying with grandchildren.

Many grandparents take the opportunity to launch into **photography** when a grandchild appears on the scene. Some grandparents use their smartphone and tablet cameras for convenient snapping. Photography buffs enjoy the time to use their expertise to build lasting memories of grandchildren's lives.

Try and keep the photos of your grandchildren in some kind of order such as labelled traditional **photo albums or online albums**. Mark with relevant information such as the names of grandchildren, the date and where it was taken.

'This is your life' style albums can make invaluable lifelong treasures for grandchildren. Grandparents are often called on to have a copy for a grandchild's **'My Life' school projects**. You can make albums for your grandchild and keep them at your home. Similarly, **moment-in-time photos** taken and processed on good quality paper will ensure your grandchildren have a lasting record of their life by the time they arrive at their 21st birthday.

Spending money

Some grandparents have a surplus of **money** while others need to manage their finances with care. Helping with special projects such as buying baby equipment or paying for music lessons for a talented grandchild can be a joy for you and a great help to the parents. On the other hand, make sure you don't over-commit yourself financially. Plus, it's important to be even-handed so as to avoid resentment among siblings and their parents.

Many grandparents are happy to give their grandchildren **spending money** for outings. They can then choose what they will spend their money on throughout the day, which can prevent constant requests for items like ice creams.

For older grandchildren, planning a **budget** can be an effective way to keep within your means when your grandchildren are in your care. The costs of recreational entertainment can quickly add up to an alarming total. Inquiring about and estimating entrance costs, family tickets, fares and parking for a planned activity will help keep your budget under control. Alternating days that involve costly activities with days filled with no-cost things to do at home or in your area is a great way to have fun and keep within your budget.

Pocket money can also be an issue when grandchildren are on a short- or long-term stay with you. Some grandparents like the idea of grandchildren learning the value of money and how to spend and save while others believe that grandchildren should gain pleasure from contributing and sharing responsibility within their home without monetary gain. There are also parents who are against the idea of children earning money until a certain age, so check with them to see what happens at home first.

Giving pocket money while your grandchildren stay with you can help your budget and give them some independence in what they spend and how they spend it. If your family agrees, it is useful to decide ahead of time whether to give pocket money or not and if chores can earn pocket money.

- First, establish what you expect your grandchildren to do without the incentive of pocket money.
- Then narrow down some chores that, given their ages and abilities, your grandchildren could do for you. Young grandchildren can earn pocket money for making beds, setting the table etc. Older grandchildren can be responsible for more complex duties.
- Are you going to pay the same rate to each grandchild no matter what their age? For example, will your seven-year-old grandchild have the same opportunities to earn what your fifteen year-old grandchild earns?
- Decide if some household chores are worth more than others or if they will all be treated equally.

- How much will you pay per job? Is there a set rate per job or is it valued according to the amount of time spent.
- If you have older grandchildren, would you organise for them to do outside jobs for friends such as taking bins in and out, cleaning windows or gardening to earn pocket money?

House rules and behaviour guidance

A few house rules can avoid chaos in your home. Gentle reminders about helping (adjusted to the ages of the grandchildren) is also a realistic expectation. Following are some examples of simple house rules and responsibilities that can help make sure everyone is relaxed and happy in your home.

- Even though you may be very familiar with each other, it is reasonable to expect a certain level of manners, such as 'Please …', 'Thank you …', 'Excuse me …' and 'May I …'
- Belongings are to be kept in designated places and dirty clothes to be placed in the washing basket.
- Food scraps, rubbish or unwanted articles to be placed in appropriate bins. Older children can help put the rubbish out or bring the bins in.
- Personal spaces and belongings are to be respected. Do not enter or play in no-go zones (for example, your study or a room containing precious ornaments).
- Keep toys in a box or basket. Expect grandchildren to pack up toys after they've finished playing. Give a reminder and help younger grandchildren with this task.
- Meals are to be eaten at the table and at set times. Help is to be given to clear the table and wash or dry or stack the dishwasher as appropriate. You may insist on saying grace or asking permission to leave the table.
- TV viewing and the use of computers and other devices will be for agreed programs and times.

- Chores will be done as a team. There should be no comments such as, 'I didn't make this mess!'
- Pets are to be treated with respect and kindness.
- Turn lights off when leaving a room.
- Limit phone calls (if they don't have their own mobile phones) and use of the internet.
- If you have limited hot water, use a timer and expect users to stick to a set time when showering. If you have a limited number of bathrooms, use a timer to make sure everyone has a reasonable amount of time in the bathroom.
- Discourage phrases such as, 'I want ...' and encourage 'I would like ...' or 'May I ...'
- Let grandchildren know that they will be asked to leave the room and find another activity if there is squabbling or arguing over minor matters.

It is easy for parents to develop the habit of doing everything for children because with busy lifestyles it can be quicker and save time. Remind yourself that you should never do what grandchildren can do for themselves. **Self-help is cool.** When grandchildren are staying with you, you can help them on the road to becoming resourceful, capable young people.

Older grandchildren can be encouraged or taught to:

- get their own breakfast
- make you a cup of tea or coffee
- plan, prepare and cook some meals
- use your microwave and the washing machine
- how to iron, mend and alter their clothes
- bring the bins in or take them out
- feed the pets
- collect the mail.

Know that **being bored is a good thing** – and actually okay in your house. This allows grandchildren the opportunity to entertain themselves. Take time off from entertaining them and encourage their creative initiative. You may be surprised with what they come up with, so be prepared to help if need be!

Individual opinions and philosophies on what is appropriate behaviour for children can create immeasurable difficulties within families. Interfering in the way a family encourages their children to learn appropriate behaviour will only cause distress. Providing supportive back-up is the best way grandparents can make life easier for both parents and grandchildren.

Many modern grandparents support the current thinking surrounding **behaviour guidance**. Rather than discipline – which is often associated with punishment in order to control children and change their behaviour – behaviour guidance aims to help children, over time, rely on adults less, guiding them as they develop their own self-control and understandng of what acceptable behaviour is.

Consistency is the basis of effective behaviour management. Whether your grandchildren are with you for the day or in your home for a short- or long-term visit, simple guidelines and limits can create a peaceful and secure environment for them. Be clear in what you expect, for example, 'We always eat and drink at the table.'

Focussing on good behaviour is very effective, too. Making a positive fuss when children display acceptable behaviour can encourage more of the same. This works really well when there is an activity involved that is of great interest to the grandchild, for example, 'Help Grandpa clean up and we can go fishing!'

✋ Tips

- Establish clear limits and boundaries and try and anticipate problems before they arise.
- Instructions need to be clear and specific. 'Pack the toys away before dinner,' is better than, 'Don't forget to clear up your mess.'
- Try and encourage children to use their own words and talk about how they feel. Avoid physical discipline of all kinds such as smacking.
- Keep calm.
- Avoid shouting.
- Avoid nose-to-nose confrontations and power struggles.
- Be flexible with routines so children are relaxed and not rushed.
- Only drive the car when grandchildren are strapped in a car seat or secured by seat belts.
- Stop the car when children fight. Let them know you will only drive when they are quiet.

If you are having difficulty with a grandchild that consistently displays **challenging behaviour**, try discussing it in a non-confontational way with their parents. This can often help, as it could be due to many reasons. Knowing ahead of time how the parents approach difficult behaviour can also be helpful. Work with your family to find the best solution for a grandchild's inappropriate behaviour and approach the situation with the grandchild in a consistent way. Don't be disheartened if it takes a few weeks for a significant improvement.

Challenging or inappropriate behaviour can frequently happen when a grandchild has become over-stimulated. Knowing the triggers, and heading them off early, is best. Calming the situation by creating a diversion to a more peaceful, alternative activity for a grandchild can also work wonders. In this case, **cool-down time** can also be used to help a child settle down and regain self control. Stay with the child and quietly talk through a solution to the problem, discussing more appropriate behaviour.

Fostering a **helping habit** when grandchildren are with you is another great way to avoid problems before they happen. It's fun for grandchildren to work with you in a cooperative team, sharing tasks such as tidying up, cooking and cleaning. Be sure to make sure your grandchildren hear and understand your requests, giving minimum instructions one at a time, and allowing them time to follow your instructions.

Tantrums

According to experts, tantrums mostly occur between the ages of two and four. This is when a toddler isn't yet able to articulate feelings such as frustration and anger. Differentiating between needs and wants can also be difficult at this age.

Tantrums have a purpose. They are designed to break down parent and grandparent resistance. They also require an audience, rarely happening when no-one is around. Tantrums usually come in two varieties: the noisy, door-slamming, floor-stomping type or the quiet, sulking variety. Speaking in a low calm voice can help. As can choosing your battles.

Communication and connection

Talking and listening are essential ways of connecting with your grandchildren. Finding time for real conversations when everyone is living such busy lives can be a challenge, but don't underestimate the potential for incidental conversations with your grandchildren while you are on the run. Chatting with babies and toddlers while they are being bathed, fed and dressed can be very special. Time spent with grandchildren preparing a meal can be a really good time to chat with older grandchildren.

Many grandparents help with walking or driving grandchildren to and from school, or to and from their after-school activities. This is an excellent opportunity to talk about 'stuff'. Grandparents are in an ideal position to model how to communicate – and connect –using good old face-to-face time. Of course, as mentioned before, using online technology such as email, Twitter, Facebook, texting and Skyping are also great ways to communicate with your grandchildren.

Conversation tactics

- Meals are great social occasions and a wonderful opportunity to have conversations with grandchildren. Make the most of these times when everyone is in the same place and glued to their seats.
- Take the lead in conversations with your grandchildren. Try and avoid direct questions straight after pick-up like, 'How was your day?' – for some reason this can often make kids clam up! Ask open questions instead. Questions that begin with, 'What …', 'Where …', 'When …' and 'How …', such as, 'What was the best thing that happened at school today?' should elicit more than a one-word answer.
- It can feel quite counter-intuitive, but children are more likely to open up if you are forthcoming about your day first, so share your own day. Laugh and talk about the best and worst things that happened to you – and they will often be keen to then do the same.
- If possible, try and make time to have one-on-one time with individual grandchildren.
- Grandchildren, especially boys, are more likely to open up and talk if they are relaxed and taking part in an activity they enjoy. So try sparking up conversations on walks or when fishing, gardening etc.

It's easy to guide grandchildren if you give **positive instructions** clearly and explicitly. Rather than saying, 'Don't fall, Joanna!' try, 'Hold on tight, Joanna!' Instead of saying, 'Please tidy up, Dylan,' try, 'Let's put the toys in the basket together, Dylan.'

Giving **firm simple requests with a justification** can make sense to even a small grandchild. For example, 'Hold my hand, Cleo, and we'll wait for the cars to go.' Or, 'Please shut the door, Benjamin. The breeze is cold on Grandpa's back.'

Being realistic and explicit in your expectations can work much better too, and head off unwanted behaviour before it begins. 'When Grandma is at the doctor's, I want you play quietly with the toys so you don't disturb other people' is much clearer than, 'I want you to be a good boy while we are at the doctor's.'

Giving instructions

- Make sure you have your grandchild's attention before giving instructions. Use your grandchild's name, squat or bend to their level to get eye-to-eye attention.
- Don't assume your grandchildren will understand your instructions. Use simple language when explaining a task. Mentally divide a task into steps and explain things one step at a time.
- Be brief. The longer you talk, the more your grandchild will be at risk of becoming 'grandparent deaf'.
- See if grandchildren can repeat what you have said.

Being polite, clear, concise and attentive in your everyday conversation – also known as **modelling** – is a great way to show grandchildren how to communicate with people they meet in their everyday life. Some other tips for communication include:

- Make your grandchildren offers they can't resist, for example, 'If you get dressed quickly, we'll go to the park.'
- Frame behaviour in a positive way.
- Be clear. 'We walk inside the house. We run outside the house.' Or, 'Please use your inside voice.'
- Praise and encourage behaviour you want to see more of.
- Don't yell. If you lose your cool, be prepared to back down.
- Give choices (but not too many at once). 'Would you rather put on your pyjamas or brush your teeth first?'
- Give and take. 'You can't go to the shops on your own, but you can play in the garden by yourself.'

Grandchildren have the happy knack of **asking questions** out of the blue. For run-of-the-mill questions, young grandchildren need short, simple, factual answers. If they need more information, they will ask for it. For older grandchildren a good reply is, 'I'm not sure, Cynthia. Let's Google that.'

Grandchildren can also have a talent for asking **difficult and tricky questions** – usually about sex. Being supportive of the parents' own viewpoints in how they raise their own children is important, as is retaining familial harmony. However, be diplomatic if you disagree with the way parents deal with their children's difficult and tricky questions. If you feel that the parents should be more forthcoming in answering children's questions – or need to justify an answer you have already given! – 'knowledge is power' is a persuasive argument, as knowledge can often provide a level of self-protection for grandchildren.

Other tricky communication issues

- A challenging argument can help older grandchildren clarify their thinking. Just make sure you don't dominate. Give your grandchildren time to present their side of the argument.
- Don't let your grandchildren play one grandparent against another. Avoid ping-ponging between grandparents, for example, 'Go and ask your grandmother … Go and ask your grandfather.'
- Don't use guilt to control grandchildren when you communicate with them, for example, 'Look what you've done to Grandpa. He's exhausted!'
- Avoid frightening threats like, 'If you pull a face like that the wind will change and you will stay like it!'
- Don't put your grandchildren down, even unwittingly. Think carefully about pet names for grandchildren as insensitive names can hurt and stay with a grandchild for a lifetime.
- Don't be afraid to apologise if you've said something you regret.

Finally, your grandchildren know everything about everything – and everyone. It's impossible to keep **secrets** from grandchildren – and asking them to keep secrets is actively discouraged by this generation of parents for sensible, protective reasons. Discuss problems clearly, simply and openly if families are going through a rough patch.

Grandparents are experts at listening. Often when a worried parent discusses problems with a sympathetic grandparent, solutions and outcomes become obvious. **Sympathetic listening** can be a great support for families, but don't rush in with remedies and good advice – it could be devastating to a parent's self esteem and the last thing a worried parent needs is some 'expert' telling them what to do. Make sure you're always available to listen in a warm, friendly manner.

Listening can be an excellent way to begin **solving problems**. If a grandchild seems quieter or develops behaviour problems, something out of the ordinary could be causing this. A parent may be ill, a marriage could be going through a shaky stage, or affections are having to be shared with the arrival of a new baby. Allowing your grandchildren the space to discuss with you how they feel can be invaluable.

Be prepared, however, that the way you see a situation may be completely different from your grandchildren's view of the same situation. Always be prepared to listen to **your grandchild's point of view** and explain your position further, even with small children. For example, you think Thomas is very dirty and in desperate need of a bath, whereas Thomas can only see that half of him is dirty and believes he only needs a wash, definitely not a bath. Humour can often come in handy to lighten these situations!

Finally, do **be careful** of anything said in haste or under pressure – a spur-of-the-moment comment, combined with a raised voice and a stern look can scare young grandchildren and their interpretation can often be faulty. Take care to elaborate if you are greeted by a puzzled, unsure look.

Celebrations

Celebrations create fond childhood memories for grandchildren. Many grandparents are celebration experts. They've conquered the art of taking something ordinary and turning it into something extraordinary. However some **family celebrations** can seem like a battleground with all the odds stacked against you.

When family togetherness wanes or the **going gets tough ... escape**. Plead an urgent business commitment or appointment you've forgotten – whatever! There will be plenty of time later when you can play the role of peacemaker and negotiator. Another alternative is to grab some company – family or grandchildren – and go for a walk to escape the celebratory ambience. There is nothing like a brisk walk to restore one's equilibrium.

Christmas and other special times of celebration can be **a time of great stress** for families for many reasons. Many grown families really don't get along. If you sense that the thought of Christmas or some other occasion looms at a time of stress for your family, gain help from counselling services. Inviting an outsider to your celebration will often provide the incentive for everyone to be on their best behaviour.

If you cannot see any hope of a pleasant time – don't go! Return visits where you will only be involved with one set of relatives at a time and you are ensured of a peaceful visit.

Tips for being a go-between

When grandchildren are involved in a family dispute between parents, such as a separation or a divorce, grandparents may be able to successfully act as go-betweens. For example, grandchildren can spend Christmas Eve with their mother and her extended family. On Christmas morning, the grandparents can meet their grandchildren somewhere and take them on to have Christmas lunch with their father and his parents.

Parties don't necessarily require large amounts of money – just time, organisation and communication. If you're a 'helper' at a family party, let the family know exactly what you'd like to contribute – perhaps the birthday cake or other food. Or will you be available for catering jobs such as setting the table, decorating the room or the last minute arranging and serving of food? Knowing your exact job description avoids complications!

Arranging a party for a grandchild can sometimes become the domain of grandparents. A party for your grandchildren doesn't have to be a celebration that breaks the budget. A successful party – one where all the young guests have a great time – can be arranged on the most modest of budgets.

If you would like the party action to take place somewhere other than your living room there are lots of options, such as the local park or zoo, where you can bring your own party picnic or barbecue. Look for a safe play area and a sheltered place to eat.

Alternatively, 'party experts' are lovely people who – as long as you can pay the bill – will provide the perfect party with food and supervised entertainment.

Party planning tips

- Invitations are nice, but often, a text or email with the details will suffice. Think about where and when to hold the party and for how long. Include a start and finish time, where the party is to be held and a contact number (two hours is about the limit for young children).
- If you're holding the party outdoors, have an alternative indoor venue in case of bad weather. What you are looking for is a place with space.
- Bite-sized pieces of whatever are your traditional dishes make great party food. Little sandwiches with healthy fillings and fresh fruit salad will be received with enthusiasm by most children.
- A cake with candles is a priority for the candle-blowing ceremony. It needs to be big enough so each child have or go home with a piece of cake wrapped in a paper napkin. Don't forget the matches and candles!
- Party games should be fun. Don't pressure little guests. Have inexpensive gifts for prizes. Make sure that everyone eventually goes home with a prize.
- Theme parties are fun for young grandchildren. How about a ghost party, teddy bears' picnic, pirates' party, a spooky party ... the list is endless. Have the table and room decorated accordingly. Extend the theme to food where possible.
- Some grandparents make fantastic party entertainers. Can you draw lightning sketches of guests, perform magic, tell great stories? How would you feel dressed up as a fairy, a clown, or a wizard? If any of these ideas appeal to you, go for it. Polish up your act! You could be a raging success. You could even go into your own party-entertaining business.
- Gently encourage your birthday grandchild to thank guests personally for their gifts.

It's a thrill to watch the delight in a grandchild's eyes as they unwrap your gift. However, **buying gifts for grandchildren** can be confusing. The power of marketing and advertising can set many a grandchild's heart on toys that grandparents wouldn't choose themselves. You need to walk a fine line. You must strike a balance between bringing joy and pleasure while avoiding toys you don't like, without causing disappointment, and getting good value for money.

Have faith grandchildren will love traditional, wrapped-up surprises and that you are the perfect person to give them. No matter what gift-giving pressures are around, you should never lose the concept of unconditional gift-giving – giving a grandchild a special token of affection.

Tips for gift giving

- No matter what toys are on your grandchildren's 'Top 10 must-have list', avoid them if you feel they've the potential to give you a nervous breakdown. If they're to be kept at your family's home, and the family are agreeable, that's a different story. Such toys could be water cannons and pistols, trucks with sirens, dolls with a limited vocabulary, whistles, drums and other musical instruments.
- Games and sporting equipment can help develop communication and social skills such as taking turns, sharing and cooperating. Do take into consideration that such gifts usually require more than one person to play.
- Avoid toys that enforce sexism, racism or violence. The classic 'violent' toy is the gun. It can be difficult to discourage grandchildren from playing with such toys but *you* don't have to buy them.
- Don't forget that granddaughters need and enjoy the experience of constructing things, and grandsons need and enjoy the experience of domestic play with tea sets, dolls, dress-ups and model kitchen equipment, too.

Handy grandparents are just the right people to **sew or build handmade gifts** such as dress-ups, soft toys, sandpits, dolls' houses, cubby houses and other suitable play furniture.

Gather together art and craft materials for a **make-and-do kit**. Depending on the materials you include, they can suit grandchildren of all ages. A make-and-do kit could contain crayons, pens, pencils, paints, adhesive tape, assortment of paper, glue, staplers, scissors, folders, Blu Tac, and paper clips. Supplies such as material, thread and needles in a sewing box can also be popular.

Think about each individual grandchild, their **interests, age and capabilities** and be aware of the grandchild's development level. If in doubt, ask shop assistants about the appropriateness of a toy. Consult with your family, but if you disagree with their recommendations or the price is out of your range, forget it. Some suggestions include:

- Selecting gifts that encourage grandchildren to use their imagination such as farm sets, dolls' houses, dress-ups and craft packages.
- Avoiding toys that leave nothing to the imagination. Some toys literally walk, talk, say what they need and what to do with them.
- Providing grandchildren with a diversity of experiences is a factor to consider. For example an outdoor toy might encourage your grandchild outside if they spend a lot of time at the computer.

Age-appropriate toys for young grandchildren

Following are some ideas for toys that are appropriate for the stage of development of your respective grandchildren.

- **Under six months** – Toys for grandchildren this age should be durable and easy to clean such as washable soft toys, rattles and mobiles. They should have no detachable parts that could be put into the mouth, nostrils or ears.
- **Six to twelve months** – At this stage, baby grandchildren can crawl or pull and reach up to furniture, stand or walk. Toddlers have poor balance and fall easily. Everything touched still goes from the hand to the mouth. Select gifts such as bath toys, nests of cubes, blocks, mobiles and cuddly toys.
- **One to two years** – Toddling grandchildren will be exploring and seeing how things work. Nearly everything goes into their mouth. Select gifts such as building blocks, ride-on toys, push-along and pull-along toys, posting boxes, picture books, lightweight balls, buckets and spades and picture story books.
- **Four to five years** – Select gifts such as simple games, paints, modelling clay and plasticene, dominoes, musical instruments and illustrated books, as well as story books that can be read aloud by parents.
- **Five to six years** – Grandchildren will be exploring, climbing, riding and enjoying games at this age. Select gifts such as kites, sewing and craft kits, carpentry kits, word or number games, swings with rubber seats, simple board games, puzzles and books.

Toys for young grandchildren need to stand up to being dropped, twisted, pulled and chewed without harming grandchildren.

- Read labels and buy non-flammable, non-toxic toys.
- Do not buy explosive or projectile toys.
- Look for information on how to use the toy and any safety equipment or batteries required.
- Dispose of packaging carefully.
- Keep young children away from older grandchildren's toys that may be dangerous for them.
- Watch for small parts that could break or come off and be swallowed or inhaled by babies at the 'anything-goes-into-the-mouth' stage for under three-year-old grandchildren.
- Teach children how to use toys – especially bikes – correctly and safely.

Giving a grandchild **a cuddly puppy or kitten can be a wonderful gift**, but it could also be disastrous for the puppy or kitten, and/or the grandchild's family. Check first with the family. Do they want their child to have a pet? Do they have a secure place to keep it? Are they willing to give the pet the care it requires? Remember the care of a pet will fall mainly on the parents' shoulders. In the case of older grandchildren, if the family is happy for a child to receive a pet as a gift, prepare your grandchild for the responsibility of caring for it.

Travelling and holidays

Family holidays with grandchildren should be a chance to unwind, have fun and spend time together in a relaxed atmosphere. Whether you are taking them on your own somewhere special, or you are all going together on an extended family holiday, a little planning can help ensure happy and successful travel experiences.

Prepare your grandchildren as much as possible for their travelling experience. Make some short trips beforehand, get in some walking practice and eat out in restaurants.

Research the places you are going to visit by watching movies and DVDs or searching the web and decide on your sightseeing-musts in advance. The anticipation of a holiday can sometimes be just as much fun as the holiday itself!

Tips for family holidays

- When travelling with grandchildren, be sure to **pack light**, use a suitcase on wheels and carry a backpack so you can keep your hands free.
- Selecting holiday accommodation where there will be other children for companionship can be a lifesaver. Resorts that cater for children as well as camping and caravan holidays are great places where grandchildren can make new friends. (But you will need to keep an eye on them at all times.)
- Make sure you arrive at your destination early in the afternoon to explore and settle in.
- Be fussy with hotel rooms. Check your room before taking your luggage to it. You'll have more bargaining power if you are holding up a queue in the hotel lobby.
- Make sure there is time for you all to enjoy some relaxing activities.
- Allocating a set amount of pocket money before the holiday begins can stop constant requests for ice creams, mini-golf etc.
- If you're feeling a bit martyrish, don't hesitate … take a day off. When you have recuperated, why not suggest that parents take a day off too while you hold the fort!
- Let your grandchildren know what will be happening every day.
- Leave some unstructured free time each day.
- Value your grandchildren's preferences for activities.

Choosing the **right type accommodation** is three-quarters of the way to a happy holiday for you and your grandchildren. There are many options for holidays with grandchildren that match a variety of budgets, whether you are taking them on your own or you are travelling as part of an extended family.

Hotels are often ill equipped to deal with families. See that you're not crammed into one room with rollaway beds and cots. If two rooms fail to provide access through an adjoining door, then a family room is the best option.

Apartments are a better choice than hotels when you're staying in the city with grandchildren. You have room to move and can cut the costs by shopping at supermarkets and self-catering.

Holiday houses are a great choice. Again you'll have room to move, and there should be an outside area suitable for play and relaxation. Self-catering is a great cost saver.

Camping and caravanning are both economical ways of holidaying with grandchildren. If you are an experienced, enthusiastic, relaxed camper, definitely take your grandchildren camping – they will just love the freedom, the back-to-basics nature of cooking and playing and the great outdoors, much like you do. This is also a great way to pass on some of your favourite activities and skills to both grandchildren and their parents. Utilising cabins in caravan parks is another excellent economical option.

Train travel is a great option for grandparents and grandchildren. There is room to move about, to sit and read, play 'quiet' games, watch DVDs, listen to CDs and play electronic games. Long-distance travel in a sleeping compartment is an exciting option to consider when you travel with grandchildren.

Air travel tips

- Today there are stringent regulations concerning cabin luggage. Check with the airline well before your departure date.
- Let your grandchildren wear their most comfortable clothes, and pack changes of clothing in your cabin luggage. Check if they can bring small, favourite toys on board.
- Take advantage of children's meals on airlines. Check if you can pack their favourite sandwich, snack, fruit and drink.
- Don't rely on the airline to provide travel activity packs for children. Check if you need to bring extra activities. If allowed, take several along, especially if you're going on a long flight.
- Strollers and baby car seats should be checked in with your luggage.

> - Give older grandchildren sweets to suck at take-off and landing to help ease the build up of pressure in their ears.
> - **Caution:** Watch grandchildren like hawks at stations, airports etc. Parents and grandparents are often distracted with finding taxis, making new connections and excited or confused children can easily walk away.

Whatever your destination or mode of transport, individual **travel survival kits** can keep your grandchildren happy and entertained throughout your holiday. Include activities with different levels of difficulty to keep your grandchildren interested.

- Finger puppets.
- Playing cards.
- Stickers.
- Activity books and puzzles.
- Pens, coloured pencils and sharpeners.
- Dice and lap-sized board games.
- Maps and a travel diary.
- Buy or borrow a portable DVD player and a selection of your grandchildren's favourite children's TV shows and movies.
- Older grandchildren can take electronic game sets.
- Portable CD players with storybook CDs provide great time-eating entertainment for small grandchildren.
- Older grandchildren will enjoy listening to their music CDs.
- E-readers can hold a library of suitable books for young grandchildren.

The-end-of-holiday blues!

Your holiday has been too good to be true! Everyone was healthy and got on famously with each other. It's been a dream of a stay till now. On the very **last day** a grandchild can become disgruntled or grandchildren start fighting and complaining. You feel miserable, lonely and rejected. Chaos reigns!

Don't worry. This is the **'we're getting ready to go home syndrome'** – the going-home transition. What has happened is that you've all been having a really good time and now your grandchildren need to let go of your care and routine and begin looking forward to returning to their own home.

Take your grandchildren's last day with you slowly. Help them to pack and prepare for the trip home. Making or buying small gifts to take home to their parents or friends can be a special part of the last day.

Encourage your grandchildren to share their feelings with you. Tell them that you understand they're looking forward to returning to their family and let them know how much you'll miss them and the special times you have shared together. Talk about **future visits**.

Naturally, grandparents can feel equally irritable – sad – when they come to the end of a pleasant stay with their family. Be gentle with yourself too, allowing yourself ample time for packing and an unhurried and peaceful journey home. Then give yourself plenty of time to settle in at home with ease – preferably in the daylight hours.

Security and safety

Safety precautions in and around your home when grandchildren are in your care don't have to be doom and gloom procedures, but the security and safety of your grandchildren is a top priority when they're with you.

You can make temporary changes to maintain a safe environment for each visit or permanent changes. As grandchildren grow older, you can reassess your home and garden. However, you will probably find new grandchildren keep arriving on the scene, and you will need constant vigilance for their safety and yours.

What could be a **hazard** in your home and garden when your grandchildren visit? Imagine seeing things from their level – what looks fun or interesting but could be a hazard? What could get damaged, even unintentionally? Take a pad and pencil as you move from room to room and list potential issues. The following list might help.

- Secure pets.
- Remove precious vases and ornaments from low surfaces or place them out of grandchildren's reach.
- Lock your study, shed and the garage.
- Clear and check the garden.
- Take medicine from bedside tables and lock them away.
- Check in the kitchen, bathroom and laundry for dangerous products.
- Stock up on appropriate food and drink.

Many safety considerations are common sense.

- Install safety switches that will cut power in an emergency.
- Use power point covers to stop grandchildren poking anything into them.
- Run cold water for a shower and bath first and then add hot water.
- Never leave grandchildren unattended in the bathroom. Have a stool or chair handy in the bathroom for you to sit on.

- Do not use portable floor-level heaters in the bathroom.
- Use cordless jugs and irons to reduce the chance of children pulling appliances on to themselves.
- Never have a hot drink when holding a grandchild.
- Check your water thermostat – 48.9 degrees is a safe temperature.
- Make sure all pot handles are turned away from the stove front.
- Avoid appliance cords that are dangling within a grandchild's reach.
- Try and keep grandchildren away from the stove or microwave when you're cooking.

Fire safety

The main causes of home fires are electrical faults and unattended cooking equipment. Most home fires occur in the kitchen, bedrooms and lounge rooms. These facts are important to remember because it is easy to be distracted when you are with young children.

- Install and maintain smoke alarms and fire extinguishers.
- Buy a fire rug and store it in a handy location.
- Plan and practise a fire drill with a home escape, for example 'If there's a fire, we'll hurry to the letter box!'
- Keep matches and flammable liquids in a safe place.
- Make sure children respond to the commands, 'Don't touch! Hot!'

Dangerous medicines and products

Many things found around the house such as cleaning products and medicines such as sedatives, tranquilisers, vitamin tablets, liquid drugs and ointments are dangerous for children.

- Install child-resistant latches on medicine and other cupboards where you store dangerous products. Store dangerous substances and products in childproof containers.

- Look for cleaning products packaged in resealable child-proof containers and keep them in a safe place. Keep cleaning products in their original containers – do not transfer them to a juice bottle, for example.
- Avoid keeping oven cleaner in the house. Buy enough for one use only and throw the container away.
- Don't keep any medication on bedside tables or in drawers.
- If you're not using medicines, return them to your pharmacist.

Safety outdoors

You will need to take steps to make a **safe outdoor environment and a secure playing space** for your grandchildren to free play.

- Clear away junk and things grandchildren might trip over. Check for sharp edges that might hurt them. Have regular household clean-ups to remove junk.
- Cut off sharp branches that hang at a child's eye level.
- Keep garages and sheds clean and keep them securely locked.
- Make sure fences are strong with no protruding nails or splinters. Secure loose boards in fences where small grandchildren could squeeze through and escape your care.
- Make sure you have childproof locks on any gate with access to the road or lanes.
- If you have play equipment such as a swing or slide, check it regularly. Make sure it is stable with no sharp edges and situated away from garden paths. Supervise play on swings so that a small grandchild cannot be hit by another swing.
- Chip bark or similar material should be under play equipment to cushion falls.
- Trampolines can be dangerous. A trampoline should be set in the ground. Only one child at a time should use it.

Pets

You need to protect your pets – cats, birds, fish and dogs – to keep them safe from inquisitive grandchildren.

Some cats or dogs are fiercely territorial and can be a risk to grandchildren. Keep an eye on grandchildren when they are around your pets. Even a friendly dog may bite. If you are unsure of your pet's behaviour around children, it's best to put your pets in a secure area when your grandchildren visit.

Check out the security if you have a fish pond and bird aviary. They can be unsafe for small grandchildren, too.

Safety on the farm

Whether you are holidaying on a farm with your grandchildren, or you live on a farm, there can be hazards that need checking. They will vary from property to property.

- Provide a safe area for playing near your house – preferably fenced off from farming activities, dams and livestock.
- Clean up old junk and remove old machinery and woodpiles where children play.
- Keep young grandchildren away from tractors and farm machinery. Supervise older grandchildren around tractors and farm machinery when they help with farm work.
- Make silos inaccessible by removing the lower steps.
- Insist helmets are worn for horse and bike riding or any motorised or moving equipment.
- Before moving machinery, check where grandchildren are.
- Store tools, chemicals and all equipment, including old machinery, well away from where children play.

Water safety

Always watch grandchildren near water. Children love water in any form. It is an enormous attraction. Think … does a small child ever walk around a puddle? Never! Most young grandchildren will have no fear of water or the ability to save themselves. Remember children can drown in as little as five centimetres of water. Pools, spas, baths, even buckets of water are hidden danger areas. Consider the following.

- Cover ornamental fish ponds with wire.
- Empty paddling pools after use.
- Supervise grandchildren in the bath.
- Don't allow grandchildren to play in the laundry or bathroom unattended.

A **safety fence** separating the house from the pool is the most important safeguard. It should always be maintained with a self-closing, self-latching gate. There should be nothing nearby that children could use to climb over the fencing or gate. In many states and countries, this is mandatory.

Outdoor spas should be fenced in the same way as swimming pools. All spas need a fixed cover. Indoor spas should have a lockable door. Like baths, empty spas of water straight after use.

Safety at the beach

Grandparents who live near the beach, or take grandchildren on visits to the beach, need to take safety precautions. Surf beaches are particularly dangerous for children. If your grandchildren haven't been in the surf before, arrange for them to have instruction from lifesavers about how and where to swim. Some lifesaving clubs run programs for children during the summer holidays.

Sun safety

Once a tan was a sign of health. Today we realise it is a sign of untraviolet radiation damage. You cannot 'toughen up' grandchildren's skin or protect them by building up a tan. As a **precaution:**

- Encourage children to play in the shade wherever possible – especially between 11 am and 3 pm daylight saving time and between 10 am and 2pm non-daylight saving time.
- Make sure grandchildren wear a legionnaire-style hat, a broadbrimmed hat or a sun visor with side flaps. They give extra protection for ears and necks.
- Grandchildren should wear loose-fitting rashies – sun-protection T-shirts, preferably with long sleeves, high neck and collar. Alternatively there is 'neck-to-knee' swimwear especially designed to resist harmful rays.
- Apply a broad spectrum, water resistant SPF30+ sunscreen regularly. Apply frequently when grandchildren are in and out of the water.
- Remember UV rays penetrate at least twenty centimetres in the water. Apply a zinc cream to lips, nose and ears.
- Make sure grandchildren wear their sunglasses when they are out in the sun.

Emergency checklists

Safety checklists are vital to protect your grandchildren, yourself, your pets and your home. In case of an emergency, you need to be aware of critical information. It's a good idea to make an emergency checklist for each of your grandchildren.

Complete the following safety and emergency checklists and place them in prominent positions when grandchildren are in your care. It's helpful to keep a copy of the emergency checklist in your wallet when you are out and about with grandchildren.

Emergency checklist

Critical information

Name: _____

Blood type: _____

Allergies: _____

Medications regularly taken: _____

Emergency phone contacts

Parents' phone numbers:

   Work: _____

   Home: _____

   Mobile: _____

Schools/preschools: _____

Childcare: _____

Police: _____

Fire: _____

Ambulance: ☎000 (national)

Nearest hospital: _____

Doctor: _____

Poisons information centre: ☎131126 (national)

Fire plan

Place to meet outside: _____

Fire extinguishers are: _____

Council: _____

Electricity company: _____

Gas company: _____

Telephone company: _____